THE VIOLET FOREST

THE VIOLET FOREST

Shamanic Journeys in the Amazon

FOSTER PERRY

BEAR & COMPANY
PUBLISHING
SANTA FE, NEW MEXICO

LIBRARY OF CONGRESS CATALOGING-IN-PUBLICATION DATA

Perry, Foster, 1960-
    Violet Forest : shamanic journeys in the Amazon / Foster Perry.
        p. cm.
    ISBN 1-879181-43-6
    1. Perry, Foster, 1960-   .   2. Healers—United States—
Biography.   3. Occultists—United States—Biography.   4.
Shamanism—Amazon River region—Miscellanea.   I. Title.
BF1408.z.F400A3   1998
291.4'092—dc21   97-52709
                                                           CIP

Cover art © 1998 by Sarah Honeycutt-Steele
Cover and interior page design: Melinda Belter
Editing: John Nelson
Printed in the United States by BookCrafters

9 8 7 6 5 4 3 2 1

*To my father
and to the Virgin Sophia
in honor of Eugenia Lyras and the creation of our dream*

Wisdom is a tree of life
for those who hold her fast;
those who cling to her, live happy lives.
Blessed is the man
who meditates on wisdom and understanding,
who builds his nest in her foliage
and spends the night in her branches,
who sets his family in her shade
and lives in her shelter.
In her glory he makes his home.

—From the Books of Wisdom and Proverbs

CONTENTS

✞

✞

✞

ACKNOWLEDGMENTS

This book is the final result of a personal journey which was influenced by numerous people for whom I am grateful: Eugenia Lyras, my partner in the Hummingbird Foundation, to whom this book is dedicated; Gerry and Barbara Clow for their encouragement, editing, and sanctuary; Dawn Eagle Woman and Bryan White, who were by my side during many of these events; Nirvan Hope, my assistant. Special thanks to John Nelson for his editing; Sarah Honeycutt-Steele for her artwork, and Melinda Belter for her cover and interior design.

During this journey, I have learned much from the late Dr. Hazel Parcells; Sondra Ray; and also from Dr. Ravi Ponniah; Dr. Linda Lancaster, Jeremy (Yakov) Scherr, Carlos Cesar de Paula, Dori and Merit Bennett; Donal Fortune and his family in Ireland; Carminha and Ian Levy and the staff of Paz Geia; Zulma Reyo, Dolores, and the whole staff of Alquimia in São Paolo; Humberto and Christina Moller and the staff of Arco-Iris in Rio de Janeiro; Samvara Bodewig and our mutual friends in Alto Paraiso; Upanishad Kessler and Sampati; Maria do Rocio Rocha (Pookie) and my friends in Curitiba; Wanda Czarlinski, Kathy Havens; Junior in Belo Horizonte; Sandra Garabedian; Dina Venancio and the staff of Editora Ground; Fernanda Freire; Miranda and Christina; Vera Maluf and family; Stellarius (Graciela Iriondo) in Buenos Aires; Diana Roberts, Rosemary Khelifa, Sue Tait in England and Ireland; Krystyna Czwartosz-Jaszcyk and her husband in Poland; Breda Bisjak and her family in

Slovenia; Madeleine Czigler in Paris; Christine Laschkolnig in Austria; Kendall and Tony Turner; Jane Tobal, Lynne Ryan; Helen Escoffier and her parents; Gail Axelrod, Skip Cowles, Sandy Satterwhite, Kathy Missell, Elaine Allen, Joan Dwyer; Raghu Markus and K.D. Kagel of Triloka Records; Andre Codrescu and the film crew of *Road Scholar*; Kevin and Gary Bobolsky; Angel Pine and Nilo Lucas; Ingmari Lamy in Sweden; Augustine Guzman in Peru; Sumeet Bali in India; Usha, Luke Gatto; and my Inner Teacher, Chiron.

A special acknowledgment and my gratitude are due to the many clients, colleagues, and friends who, over the years, have taught me through the openness of their healing journeys. Finally, I would like to express my deepest love for the spirit of the hummingbird, who sits at the fulcrum of the Universal Tree and guides and directs these words.

INTRODUCTION

For the past five years, I have traveled around the world and have recorded, through spirit and with deep feeling, the events here related. An unseen hand with great tenderness has guided me through many difficult transitions. *The Violet Forest* is a mythopoetic account of those travels; it is my attempt to understand the spiritual hand that guides us when we enter the unknown and are forced to sacrifice old ways of thinking and living. The outer journey through the Amazon jungle described in this book is more importantly an inner search to find a place in the world, a home. Nothing could prepare me for the wildness of the Amazon, the ayahuasca journeys of Peru, the passion of Brazil, or the overwhelming nature of my own purification by Spirit. I wanted to be initiated through travel, to understand why for two thousand years pilgrims came to Eleusis in Greece to be initiated. To face my inner daimons and experience what that ancient Greek soul remembered was an integral part of my quest.

Since childhood the darkness of the forest has been my sanctuary. Only by facing my fears, alone, in the shade of trees, did I feel empowered and ready to face the difficulties of life. The Violet Forest is a world of imagination and a place of calling and healing. In this rendering, the forest is violet because by owning any experience in life we become exalted. No experience leaves us the same. The color violet is noble, introverted, yet courageous in communicating the exaltation of the unseen, of that tender hand of the divine guiding us to see our experiences through the soul's eyes.

In this account I am searching for the beauty and silent wisdom that lives in the natural world. I want the spirit of the forest to talk through me and to guide all of us to a deeper understanding of the challenges we face in life and of how to put ourselves in the service of humanity. From the beginning, we participated in the life of trees. Trees cared for us and taught us wisdom. The tree for children is another world, a place of freedom, security, where all their dreams become real. Children climb, hide, sit in, hang from, and build houses in trees. Here the imagination is released, and children can heal their loneliness or pain.

The tree's strong presence allows the child to feel real solitude. I remember letting the tree take charge, watching how it gave refuge to the world of squirrels, birds, and insects. It felt safe to rest into the curve of the tree, to take in the smell of resins, and to explore the mystery all around it. I had to return to the forest to reclaim the beauty of apples, plums, pears, pine nuts, hazels, and almonds. I understood the Greek writer Nikos Kazantzakis when he declared, "I saw the world as a tree, a gigantic poplar, and myself as a green leaf clinging to a branch with a slender stalk."[1] My soul was like an acorn, the seed that would grow, mature, die, and be reborn.

The Violet Forest brings each of us closer to the whole of nature, the sensitivity of natural rhythms, the secrets that only a tree can hold for a child, in memory. Throughout my life, trees have absorbed my loneliness, anxiety, bruised emotion, and have given me shelter and comfort. The branches of willows and weeping birches were all havens for my escape into privacy. I felt the blessings of wise, vast-spreading branches, of the friend-ship of the locust tree, the juniper, magnolia, acacia, oak, elm, elderberry, catalpa, and holly. In the crown of a tree, I became a child of Earth, oriented toward heaven. I never can be a mere spectator of trees; I must enter into them, put my own existence in order in their serenity. They are strength, longevity, greatness, and the order captured in the heart. In trees I found that life is a great unity, a cyclic order that creates and destroys. Through evolving and dying, encompassing birth and decay, the tree is the symbol of this book.

This book is the wild forest of my experience, which contains many difficult and harsh moments. I healed my own pain and wounding through this book, and it is my intention that you do as well. I found *The Violet Forest* writing me after I visited my childhood home and discov-ered that every tree had been cut down and my family's old house destroyed. This thrust me back into the past and my woundedness as a boy. The love of that forest had sustained my difficult transition from a boy to a man. This experience threw me back into the absence of love in childhood.

Jung said that love is the absence of power. My life has been spent in seeking power, in the will, and in the attainment of ambition. I have come to realize that the sole ambition underlying this quest has been to receive love from a person, a thing, nature, and stubbornly to see love when it is not present. I have fought an enemy, an evil, to know its opposite, and to cleanse my mind of duality. I have fought with love to know the difference between narcissism and nihilism, and to express love with detachment and emptiness. A great lesson of life is to express love regardless of the outcome.

There is a hand reaching out over a chasm in a dream, and we must take that hand. There is suffering, fear, and trembling before anything new can come in or before the moment of death. Yet among the dying, in the act of dying, most people become compassionate, caring, and empty of selfishness. One day we just know everything will be all right, and we trust, we have a moment of letting go, and we enter reality.

Life, the Deep Feminine and the Deep Masculine, is an abyss. This abyss has no bottom. So leap, jump, fly, embark, and dive into this pool. Create your own grounding for a time because grounding is temporary, fleeting, and impermanent. Let day-to-day awareness, as a practice, be your guide. There is no right way to feel interbeing or interconnectedness. Find a practice that suits you and commit to it with boldness and with genius, and stay with the emptying and gathering of self, like the phases of the Moon. *We are all on course.* The next step always presents itself.

Stand in the intersection and be quiet at the center of the noise. Be in the darkness of the Amazon and become a candle. Stand in the midst of loneliness, when tears and laughter are the same thing, and feel the one you know inside. There comes a moment in life when all your old ideas and concepts are no longer valid or real; they undergo a million shatterings, and you simply say, "I don't know." That is a great moment of inquiry as you wait for the new. You become the object of the search at that point. You are That. Seen and unseen. Inner and outer. This and That. I and You. Atman is Brahman.

Accept being the son or daughter of woman, and also be the son or daughter of God/Goddess. Live in both worlds. Put your feet in both realities, become practical, have a practice, have a community of peers to keep you on track, and dive deeply into silence and the no-self. Give yourself time every day for silence, for attention, for no-mind, for relaxation—to release the notion of self—and then go into the world. The world's mirror will project to you the tests and beauty you need. A time for work, a time to contemplate.

Buddha said that life is a bridge. Do not build your house on this bridge. Home is not in the past. It is what you are moving toward. It is what you finally come to embody. Mindfulness, attention to the inner self, and the inner sounds of the body in meditation are ways to be still and find home. Another involves stillness in nature, breathing to still the heartbeat and emptying to know another reality beyond the ego's fictions. Another is to meditate with your eyes open, with awareness of your inner and outer surroundings at the same time.

I am in the search for home inside, in the mystery and reality and fiction of the inner life. I am the object and subject of that search. I am it and it is not me. I am the self and the no-self. In that sense, through inquiry and questioning I can be free and know the nature of love.

Come on this journey with me to a Violet Forest. That is an image of my home, my soul, and the soul of the world; it is vibrant and violet, and the forest of the body, this forest and jungle of the Amazon, this inner jungle of the painter Henri Rousseau.

PROLOGUE

Chiron and Rousseau

For Rousseau, landscape is not houses or mountains or virgin forest; it is man walking in wonder among the trees.[1]

—Roger Shattuck

Wandering through the Museum of Modern Art in New York City at age seven, I saw a painting of a luminous red sofa sitting in the middle of a jungle. The painting, *La Reve* or *The Dream*, is an image of Henri Rousseau's first female lover reclining in one of his imaginary jungles. Only a child could understand this dream-reality. I stood in front of that painting as if I had discovered a lost treasure—a new way of seeing. Rousseau explained to art critic Andre Salmon, "You shouldn't be surprised to find a sofa out in virgin forest. It means nothing except for the richness of the red. You understand, the sofa is in a room; the rest is Yadwigha's dream."[2] He went on to explain that the simple power of Dream dictated the scene to him. Like a child, he spoke only of the compelling reality of Dream and painted what he saw. I entered a greater reality that day and saw my own inner dream—the forest of possibility within the soul.

The French painter Henri Rousseau's jungle landscapes and tropical flora and fauna did not come from his direct experience of the Amazon but from his visits to the Jardin des Plantes in Paris; he had traveled only in a waking dream to these exotic landscapes. Within the borders of his paintings, wild beasts and human beings partake in the all-absorbing presence of nature. Roger Shattuck wrote of him, "Rousseau's finest paintings convey the ominous and alluring atmosphere of the riddle and form a haunting image of the spiritual in art . . . a mystery that keeps two half-dancing carnival figures alone in the moonlight, that keeps a glaring lion poised over a Negroid gypsy in the desert, that keeps a festoon of snakes docile before the music of a flute player."[3]

For me, Rousseau inhabits his paintings like I inhabit my dreams. In childhood I dreamt of the jungles of Brazil, using my inner eye to transform my backyard into a wild, thick forest. Rousseau transformed his world through the act of painting it. After my brief visit to the museum, I attempted to do the same through my dreams of the jungle.

As an adult I am reminded by Rousseau never to lose the faith and imagination of a child. I have learned to respect my sensitivity and to teach others to do the same. My dream of the Violet Forest is the landscape of my own sensitivity with which I wish to change the world. Rousseau was my first teacher because of the singularity of his vision and the mysticism inherent in his art.

I have discovered that there are three realms of existence. The middle realm is where we live this earthly life, bound by linear time and by three-dimensional space. Above is the celestial realm and below the infernal realm of the Underworld. To move with poise through these realms, holding a balance between opposites from which to create cosmos out of chaos, is my spiritual destiny. I feel that we must begin to identify this middle realm as a dream and learn to shape it like a lucid dream.

Henri Rousseau gave me the first inkling of how one could see through the inner eye and heart, but more importantly, through his voice I could hear the forest inside. As I grew older, suffering replaced innocence, and my search for meaning and acceptance came through my discovery of Chiron.

Chiron was a centaur in Greek mythology, half horse, half human. Unlike other centaurs, who were descended from Ixion or Centaurus, Chiron was the son of the Titan Cronus and the nymph Philyra and was immortal. He also differed from other centaurs in his nature. Centaurs were known for their unrestrained habits, their untamed sexuality, but Chiron was one of the wisest and learned of living beings. Some of the greatest Greek heroes were sent as children to his remote cave on Mount Pelion for instruction. Among his students were Jason, Asclepius, Actaeon, and Achilles.

Chiron was noted for his knowledge of surgery and the other medical arts. He was a wise prophet, teacher, musician, and artist, who was adept at archery, hunting, the arts of war, ethics, religious ritual, and natural science. He had begun to map the heavens and is said to have originated the medicinal use of plants. He is sometimes credited with inventing the musical pipe and the spear.

A wall painting from the Basilica of Herculaneum depicts Chiron teaching Achilles to play the lyre. Here, he is a wise foster father teaching a man of courage about music. Achilles learned about the ancient virtues from

Chiron: contempt for worldly goods, a horror of lying, a sense of moderation, and resistance to evil passions and grief. I longed for a father who would be my teacher, a mentor of the caliber of Chiron; I searched for him inside my psyche, inside my dreams.

Years after discovering Rousseau, I had my first definitive dream of Chiron. It begins in a small chateau near Saints Maries-de-la-Mer in France. I am an older man coming to terms with his own self-chosen pain, the patriarch of a large French family with aristocratic pretensions in the mid-nineteenth century. My wife has died of cholera, and my heart is grieving her. I want to die after my wife's passing, and the sharp wound of my loneliness draws me into the arms of a Gypsy woman. I choose to share my bed with a woman I could not marry, one who loved to dance in her red dress during our family's many parties. I need her companionship to fill the void of my mourning, and I desire her sexuality to give me a thirst for life.

This Gypsy woman speaks to me in the dream about drinking a bitter poison in the silence of a forest. I feel her words as she calls out for a physician to heal my sick self. She is calling for an inner physician from the depths of my soul to restore me. I have forsaken God and have no clear reason to live. My heart is heavy, hard, and distrustful. I fear that without love and the desire to live, the Gypsy and everybody else will take advantage of my vulnerability and divest me of my money. In the dream, I sleep with the Gypsy woman on numerous occasions and have two children with her. I feel betrayed by the feminine, abandoning myself to a Gypsy woman, unable to forgive God for taking my wife. I am consumed by guilt for these illicit children that I cannot care for.

In the next scene, I am older with short gray hair, riding in a boat and carrying the statue of a Black Madonna. I still feel guilty for not loving the Gypsy's children as much as my wife's and for not honoring her memory. I cannot surrender this pain to God, and my wound will not allow healing to enter. I refuse to release the past, my body's bent over in shame. Hundreds of Gypsies surround the boat as part of a Gypsy festival. I stand erect in the center of the boat and hold up the Black Madonna in exultation for all the Gypsies to see and to supplicate. At that moment, I lose my balance and fall clumsily overboard into the sea, clutching the statue. The sea plays tricks on my eyes, turning a violet color as I invite in death. I know that in the future the statue will be found at the bottom of the water, but I wonder if my soul will free itself from my body. The last image I see while drowning is that of a centaur. He shows me his hoofs in the shape of the crescent Moon and says, "Mare, Mater, Mother, look to land and forest." He looks exactly like the wall painting of Herculaneum—robust, alert, and patient. He has learned compassion from his suffering, and looking into his eyes I find the same relief. The centaur places his hand over the wound in my heart, but it is futile because, to be healed, I must die first. My lungs are flooded with water; I surrender to death and drown. I die knowing that this is the physician who can heal my wounds through his touch.

I have since searched for his tender, unseen hand to bring me out of an abyss of buried memories. I know that

I must wake up from this dream and rescue myself from the bottom of the ocean, the sea of my origins, and return to find him. In later dreams, I remember voluntarily surrendering to death, but I cannot feel the return to the Earth Mother, to her healing embrace. I see only the terrible Goddess in her rejecting, destructive form. A lost part of my soul was left there in the depths and has to be brought back.

I looked for the centaur in my father because he was a physician. In his compassion for his patients, I searched for the healer within me. I expected him to teach me music, about hunting and poetry, and how to follow my instincts. In this search for a father, I could only see my own wounds, and my expectations of my father were unrealistic.

As a child I felt deeply wounded by my parents. My mother gave up her creativity and her career to raise children. My father was absent, involved deeply in his own work. Feeling lonesome I sought refuge in the forest behind our house in New York State. Once I fell asleep under a mimosa tree and woke up with the conviction that humanity had originated with the first tree, and that when the last tree is cut down, human beings will become extinct. I believed that the world began in water, in the ocean. I struggled to make peace with the water of life, fearing that I would drown in the Great Mother or in my own personal mother's anxieties. I could not separate from either the personal or collective mother to become a separate self. Trees became my one way of standing tall to take in the wonder of life without being overwhelmed or invaded.

Chiron became an imagined presence in my adolescent dreams, urging me not to rise above human life and my human father, but to embrace them. Chiron urged me to have compassion for my own neglected suffering and to be aware of my own mortality. Only through facing this wounding with my father could I discover my true responsibility to others, my character, and my calling.

Chiron's own wounding occurred when the hero Hercules was invited by the centaurs to dinner. An argument interrupted the dinner, and Hercules began to fight the centaurs. During the ensuing confusion, one of his arrows struck Chiron in the leg. The wound, inflicted by Hercules, a past friend of his, was untreatable and unbearable. He suffered for the rest of his immortal life. Chiron represents a battle between our two halves: the lower, rejected animal part, and the human part. His wound is the age-old repression and persecution of our instinctual selves. The working out of Chiron's unique destiny offers hope for healing our own wounding.

Before Chiron's birth as the son of Cronus (Saturn) and the nymph Philyra, his mother protected herself by changing into a mare to escape from the eyes of Cronus. He was searching through Thessaly for his baby son Zeus, whom his wife Rhea had hidden away to protect him from being devoured by his father. Cronus pursued Philyra and changed himself into a horse and mated with her. Chiron was born with the body and legs of a horse and the torso and arms of a man. At his birth, his mother, disgusted at his body, pleaded to be changed into anything other than a mare. The gods turned her into the linden tree, and Chiron was subsequently abandoned.

Apollo found the child and became his foster father, teaching him numerous skills.

Chiron's birth is significant because he was conceived while his parents were in animal form, from pure instinct. Spurned by a mother who rejected her own instinctual side, Chiron was torn by self-rejection. A negative, rejecting mother coupled with an absent father forged Chiron's destiny at a very young age as an outsider from society. He had to face his feelings of abandonment, this break from both the mother and father, to find his destined path as a teacher and physician.

Chiron was raised by a very civilized foster father, Apollo, the god of music, prophecy, poetry, and healing. Apollo's reason and education were the antithesis of Chiron's instinctual side as a centaur. With Apollo as his mentor, Chiron was compelled to reject his unbridled instinctuality in favor of culture, order, creativity, and Apollonian ideals.

Chiron was released from his suffering through exchanging destinies with Prometheus, who had been bound to a rock for eternity by Zeus. This was his punishment for mocking the gods and for his theft of fire. Prometheus had defied them, as we all must do when retrieving a part of our individual selves from the unconscious. He stole the fire of the gods to bring the light of consciousness to the darkness of humankind. He was a pioneer who not only stole from the gods but also had to learn to respect them with humility. Zeus decreed that Prometheus could only be released from his punishment if an immortal agreed to take his place. Chiron volunteered and relinquished his immortality. After his death came his resurrection as the constellation Centaurus (or Sagittarius), and Prometheus was freed on the condition that he would always wear a ring and a crown of willow leaves. This was to teach Prometheus humility: the ring to remember the past, and the willow as a tribute to Chiron's death for his sake. Prometheus gained his freedom by Chiron's sacrifice. And Chiron was healed by retreating to the Underworld and facing his mortality.

The planetoid Chiron was discovered in 1977 at the Hale observatories in California. The discovery of a new outer planet is an important event for astronomers and astrologers alike, ushering in a new archetypal pattern, a face of the divine acting on the collective psyche. Chiron's position between Saturn and Uranus symbolizes the form and tradition of society—Saturnine conservatism and structure—and on the other hand the desire to destroy and rebel against structure in the name of freedom—Uranian individuality and progress. Poised between the two, Chiron embodied a solution for me. On one hand, he was calling my soul to be socially responsible and aware of my limits, aware of my need to be a victim or inflictor, and aware of my tendency to rescue others as a healer. But Chiron was also affirming my personal commitment to my own growth and preservation of soul and identity.

I discovered that Chiron, as the archetype of the Wounded Healer, was preparing me to face my own suffering, to not project it on others through resentment and jealousy. Owning my own suffering initiated my healing journey. It rooted me to the Earth and to the shared suffering of others, and it urged me to fulfill my individuality through service to others. I could not be complete in myself until I had embraced my own woundedness—only then I could embrace the woundedness of others.

Subsequently, I went on a quest to find meaning through my outer experiences in the world. I wanted to actualize the paintings of Rousseau and return to the jungle, to the instinctual part of my nature. I wanted to ride horses and be one with them, not abuse and reject them because I feared losing my own power. I desired to break away from the assembly of gods (society)—like Prometheus stealing the fire—and find my own inner teacher and authority. I literally searched for my father in the Violet Forest of my dreams; I actually went to the Amazon to heal my relationship with him. What does it mean to be a man, to be a father, and to meet the Father God? This search for wholeness first led me to a spiritual father named Tserete, to his tribe, and to the chirotic center of Brazil.

THE VIOLET FOREST

PART ONE

Death of the Fathers

CHAPTER 1

The Xavante Indians

José Luis Tserete is a fierce warrior chief of the Xavante tribe in Matto Grosso, Brazil. The original name of the Xavante is Auweuptabi. I met him in Rio de Janeiro in 1993, and he said to me, "My fight is invisible. It is spiritual." He is proud, fatherly, an orator who speaks to the 130 people in his tribe before the dancing begins at sunset. He honors the day with respect for his land, for his home, and for his survival.

Fifty years ago his tribe numbered 100,000 people. Multinational corporations then bought the Xavante land (roughly the size of the Netherlands). In 1952, according to Tserete, these groups airlifted clothes contaminated with smallpox into the Xavante villages. Thousands of Indians died, even the proud warrior Xavante. The Xavante were nearly wiped out by smallpox; the stunned survivors, lost without their people, crossed the River of Death (the actual name of the river), where they found a priest. He had a mission to educate the Indians and many were converted. This priest later abused his power through sexual misconduct and through his blind need to convert the Indians to Catholicism.

Although Tserete survived this disaster, he could not properly eat for 15 years because of the pain in his heart. He wants his tribe to again number 100,000. He still has the anger, the invisible war. But he has decided to revive the old ways of the tribe, the ways of his childhood and of the first village. He told me that there is only one Xavante left who knows how to make ceramic pots in the old way. The skill will die with her if it is not taught. Now there are only the 130 people in the San Felipe village near Campinapolis.

He showed me the sacred lake in which no one ever swims. It is a place of emergence, pristine and turquoise. Next to the lake is the sacred cave of his people, where they once had picnics and a few ventured deep inside. There the Xavante would converse with the people of the inner city below the cave. They met advanced teachers who showed them how to gather roots, herbs, and plants, and how to understand the stars.

The chief gave me three plants. One was a root called *uhotetepa*, which cures cancer, ulcers, wounds, and back-ache. Another root is called *watopiri* and it heals AIDS. He instructed me on how to take care of this root and how to replant it in the United States. The third root is a pro-tector. It is called *iwaipo*, and it is slightly cut four times on the side. He said the root is connected to the rain and the stars. These roots are my presents. They give me sus-tenance from Earth, and a strong foundation.

He also wrapped a thin cord made from tree vines around my wrists and ankles to ward off disease.

I met Tserete in a tiny apartment near the *favellas*—the slums governed by corrupt police and drug lords—after a huge storm had pelted Rio de Janeiro, toppling trees, washing the air of violence, and settling the sky with seven complete rainbows over the city.

When I saw Tserete behind the open door, smiling,

regal, I felt a great meeting was afoot. The two of us shared spiritual energy. That is the only way I can describe the exchange. I sang an old welcoming song for him. He ordered me to lie down, and he passed the palm of his hand over my belly, calling up the force of blood, of healing warmth. I felt a light shiver of blessing filling my body, my soul becoming enlarged. I was home. He knelt next to me and shared his life force with me, shaman to shaman, in humility and in respect for the gift of spirit. He chanted in Xavante with a deep, brooding sound from the gut, which was directed, strong, and fearless. I watched my fear leave, love for his soul, his tribe, and honor for my body and his, remaining.

He told me about a dream. He was in his home in the forest, a large round house of straw, dreaming of an Indian man—or was he part Indian and white, he could not tell, except for the nature of his one heart. He had seen me in this dream and knew the work that was coming through me, and he had come to Rio to find me. He also saw that I would help his tribe and would bring him to the United States. North America is very far away to the Xavante, a land of promise, of wealth. He knew little of the real United States and the plight of Native Americans. We had our meeting under the rainbow warrior sky and set a date for my arrival in Matto Grosso.

After the decimation of his tribe by the U.S. multinationals, my coming in peace to their village would be symbolic—a reconciliation from an old war. For them I symbolized a new, better country. He wanted me to leave the city, to feel at home on his reservation. I went.

It took three long days to drive to the reservation. I

came with my friend Humberto, my interpreter for the journey, and my driver, Bruno, in a large Toyota with four-wheel drive. The sun was hot, steamy, the roads pockmarked with holes, and we had endless hours to contemplate the meaning of the journey. We passed prostitutes on the road waiting to seduce the truckers. They came from small villages and had families but needed extra money. They disguised themselves with multicolored wigs. We passed endless *eros* hotels and *chuchascarias* or meat houses. In spite of this distraction, I felt a connection to Xavante land, an invisible silver thread moving me closer to it. I arrived in Campinopolous exhausted from the drive and eager to see Tserete's face, like a prodigal son awaiting his father. But we could not locate him anywhere. We asked around town, but no one knew his whereabouts. We had missed our rendezvous by a day. Where did he live? The San Juan reservation? Humberto got directions and Bruno took us directly to the tribe, bypassing the chief, Tserete. This was our first mistake.

It was disrespectful not to meet him first. I found this out too late. We drove under a huge canopy of trees to the side of a river with a large fallen tree straddling the two sides of the banks. The tree was wide, the bridge from our world to theirs. I stepped out of the car, took off my shoes, and crossed the tree bridge to the other side. Standing there were fifty Xavante youth who were radiant, muscular, muddy, and curious. They had been waiting twenty-four hours in red body paint for me to arrive and for them to begin the ceremonies of welcoming.

I knew them somehow, knew their inner names.

What was I doing here in this world of theirs, so strange and yet so familiar? Tserete was still waiting for me in town. I sent Humberto to find him—another mistake. To show respect I should have gone to town and found him myself. Instead, I sat in the village, where children with ashen faces played with my clothes, and talked with two people I knew from Rio.

Paul and Deborah had come to a workshop of mine in which Tserete was at my side, doing his profound healing work. He had asked Paul and Deborah to join us. I greeted them on my arrival, but they were sad, different than their usual selves. They told me of *sarna*, a disease contracted from the hair of the dogs, and how the dogs here were mistreated. They told me women were subordinate, and the water was unsafe to drink. The Xavante homes were shared with roosters, animals, and many family members lived together in a small space with no sanitation. Westerners expect to find the noble savage living in pristine innocence. I had spent too much time on Native American reservations to have such expectations.

Tserete finally arrived, upset, wounded in his pride. I apologized and gave him my gifts at once, hoping to appease the gods. He was human, generous, and forgave quickly with the swipe of his hand and a few utterances. It was safe again.

We danced the circle dance with the whole tribe— Bruno, myself, Humberto, Paul, and Deborah. The women jumped forward and backward, the men feet together, then feet apart. The songs were deep, throaty, like the roar of a bull. The children made fun of us when we missed a beat and lost our footing. They teased us without judgment and Paul became their clown. It was a celebration of community, of mutual survival, and a meeting of worlds. I was glad to be there.

I was the guest of honor. At sunset I had to address the whole tribe like an orator in the Roman Senate. Everybody sat on dried palm fronds on the bare earth. Their faces told of hard work, respect for Tserete, mixed with a mild nonchalance. They felt my heart expand to take in their feelings, hurts, in the common language of sorrow, suffering, and beauty. I told them my path was the beauty way, a way of pollen, a path for the hummingbird—or in Portuguese language, *beija-flor*. I finished my speech. The words were not awkward though I felt awkward. Communication with no translation. It was from the heart, the only medium for unspoken language.

In the following days, we ate rice and beans and played volleyball with the children. While Humberto played soccer, I walked in fields of guava, corn, rice, bananas, and beans. Tserete took me to the sacred cave and the tunnel that led to the inner Earth—before an avalanche closed this connection to their teachers there. They now spoke to the stars and by telepathy to the inner Earth intelligence.

The cave was pitch black, filled with obsidian bats screeching and droning. The entrance was vast, a wide opening into Earth, like an ear. I listened to the iron crystal core of the planet, the ringing of Earth's eardrum. The cave felt alive, like being in the womb; the bats were tiny fetuses waiting to emerge from inside that belly. The cave had the primeval smell of bat droppings, rotting wood, and ancient fires. And it was as black as the Black

Madonna, the Dark Mother.

Next to the cave was the sacred lake, azure colored, where no one was allowed to swim. The lake embodied a story, a song of the origins of the Xavante. The story involved a beast, the birthing of twins, and an animal leaving the lake. It told of an ancient woman and her offspring. Tserete told me their creation story, and I felt it was my own.

The tribe had a special child, a boy, who was being groomed to be chief one day. He was the offspring of Tserete and a woman from the Pleiades who had visited him. The Xavante told this story plainly, the mystery hidden in the silence between words. The boy looked ordinary enough, but I could see that he was Tserete's chosen. He had the burden of the future, of the hero, in his blood: part god, part human, like the rest of us. Time would reveal his fate and the destiny of his tribe.

These were great honors not lost on me. I bought the tribe meat to feed everyone and foodstuffs like rice and beans, and later a bicycle. Tserete needed a truck, but a truck costs $35,000. I would not give in to Indians wanting money, more money, and another truck. I had to learn to stop giving materially and to give in other ways.

There was always that fear, the thought of being used, that I was the rich American who would save the tribe financially. I had to learn to say No!, to have limits, to come spiritually open and to give with an open heart, to help with respect and without feeling guilty; I did not want to give money instead of love. In fact, every truck they had ever received was wrecked after only a few years of use. Although they had a mechanic, they did not know how to take care of their precious trucks. Many Xavante would come up to me in town earnestly asking, "Can you buy us a truck?" in the same way they would ask for ice cream.

This was the hardest part. To be true to myself and to let them have their pride, their fierce spirit, and to honor the women in the tribe despite any patriarchal overtones. Women needed to have their place of authority and to make more executive decisions. I knew this occurred in the confines of their homes, but it needed to be brought out in the open, away from secrets.

Meanwhile, the boys fought with clubs in a ritual ceremony. It made the boys tougher, but the clubs were hard, rough bone. Children bled in these games while their families wiped the tears away. The Xavante men are the strongest warriors, the last to be decimated because of their stubborn will. They are heroes, larger than life, and macho.

Unfortunately, most of South America has the macho mentality and the dominator virus. My role has always been to be a man but to be aware of the feminine at all times. The Great Mother is whom I serve. She gives us the strength and humility to respect death as a companion and to embrace it in defeat. The samurai always wins because he neither wins nor loses in his mind before the battle. He is unattached to the outcome; he therefore always wins.

Those children were the keepers of a tradition, whether right or wrong. I made no judgment and was just the witness of a culture fighting for its life. This masculine strength was what I often lacked in my own experience. Here I found an acceptance of a deep masculine tradition. I watched children in school learning the old ways, the stories, and the Portuguese language. They were eager both to be Xavante and to know the outside world beyond the river. Tserete was their bridge and hope.

He was a chief and it was his calling. He once told me that, whenever he leaves the tribe for more than a week or two, someone dies—the thread begins to break, so fragile is the link of souls. He was like my father, ruthless and compassionate, doing the best he could, but blinded by his own human limitations. He was the next step for his tribe, slowly creating a future for them after they had lost almost everyone. He had to be a source of hope.

I found out that he traveled extensively to know the white world and to make alliances. Treaties were often broken, and to him the Funai, the government Indian Bureau, was corrupt or inept. And although *Doctors Without Borders* was a helpful health organization, Tserete wanted to bring back the old ways of prayer, herbs, and roots. He did not want allopathic medicine to heal the sarna. He was their shaman with four other elders, each versed in a specialty—stars, herbs, trees, plants, roots, the healer of bones, the keeper of songs, etc. He did not want white medical doctors showing him how to take care of his tribe.

One morning it was my turn to give the tribe a gift of healing. Tserete had come to my workshops in Rio and worked by my side to help people heal themselves shamanically. He sang and pulled wounds of the heart out of people's bodies with hand gestures and chants. He worked with cancer and AIDS patients, giving them herbs and roots that built a spirit bond to the Earth. He made his own version of medicine bundles and had his own honoring of the four directions and the ancestors.

The tribe laid two people before me for healing and then made a wide circle around us. The Xavante were used to quick, fast healing. Not giving into their impatience, I took my time. First, a girl was sitting on my lap, lost in thought. She needed a soul retrieval. I told the tribe that I saw her conception, the identity of the spirits talking to her, and her trauma. She began to cough while I searched with my animal guides for her soul. All my helpers had to assist on the inner intuitive planes. As her soul returned fully to her body, after the release of trauma, I knew I had struck a good bargain with her ancestors. I had asked Archangel Michael to help lift an old curse from her conception. Another woman had cursed the mother while she was pregnant, obviously jealous and envious of her conception. This young girl was the unwilling victim of that woman's curse or conscious negative thoughts.

She was a changed girl after the healing work, as if she had awakened from a long dream of suffering. The atmosphere became different after I had passed this test; like the little girl, the whole tribe began to blossom and be receptive. I saw her past lives, her sorrow in the last life, and her painful death. This blew away in the wind after a brief talk with her soul. She needed my total attention and that is what gave her the desire to live. Someone had to care for her with a deep love, someone foreign, new to the tribe, and this brought her out of her fantasy of having to feel unique and special.

After that she followed me around the village smiling. I understood her being an outcast, saw her value in the tribe. Only Tserete had seen as much. I was there long enough to honor her slow-growing, independent streak. I wanted her to develop a sense of "I" consciousness to counterbalance the tribal group soul. Each person is honored in the tribe. There was a crazy man who was venerated but had to be told when to leave, as he followed and accosted Bruno repeatedly. I felt that one woman was a profound healer and took her by a reluctant hand into the center of the circle and made her work by my side, even though she tried to run away, ashamed.

The second healing involved a young male warrior with sarna. His skin was gray-white ashy, his eyes bloodshot like a dog's. He moved slowly, with little energy, insects crawling on his open wounds. Sarna is a highly contagious disease transmitted by animals, and it was unsanitary, dangerous to touch his skin. My soul said to touch him, hold his back, to not show fear. That was his healing: for me to be fearless and not to avoid him, and to tell the story of his sexual contact by the drinking hole with a woman and his guilt of self-rejection. He had committed some sexual taboo in his tribe that no one knew, but he carried his shame, his grief, and his self-judgment. A healing is a healing of the mind, an appeasement to the god of the mind, to reconcile mind with heart and body.

I announced his "sin" to the tribe, his secret, and forgave him. He also carried the same sexual proclivities as his father. He carried his father's shame and secrets. I felt a rush of subtle energy up my spine as I worked on him; the energy of the ethers ran through my hands to warm him. This energy comes from clearing the chakras and allowing the spirits of wisdom to dance up the body parallel to the spine. I began to visualize colored light, angels around his body, and then I saw the sarna, his disease, leave. The darkness, like spots in the auric field, began to fade completely. I felt a kinship with him and a respect; it was not his time to die, or to give up. He was acknowledged. The burden of his genealogical karma was ending. The disease left his body in three days.

Everyone in the tribe seemed pleased, more aware. But I also felt that this was routine for them, just yet another healing ceremony. I started to feel less and less estranged, and saw the commonality of human beings. After my morning healings, the whole tribe lined up to hold me. Each person wanted to embrace me and to listen, through the interpreter, for what I had to say. That is the moment you become an agent of love. You step out of the way of the current and become a fierce channel of the divine. I let go into a vast reservoir of energy that always moves through my four bodies with a calming, soothing release of tension and indecision.

I held a hundred people in my arms that day, saw the fate of each one, how each was placed in the order of things. Through interpreters, I gave each a message. I could see through the eyes of the children their future marriages, their personal destinies within the tribe, and I had to discuss it with them and Tserete for verification.

The oldest Xavante man looked into my eyes, invited me into the tribe, and placed a rope made from a tree

vine across my wrists. One elder wrapped the rope firmly around my hand, tightly tying the rope eight times and
then three times underneath for protection. I was given
gifts—basket, a necklace of shells, feathers, and was
accepted into the tribe as a kind of ambassador. That
was the beginning of a deeper bond.

On the last day, the men took me to their sacred
grove of trees. The trees were violet in the shade. (The
trees shade us to make our colors deeper.) We smoked
there and sang, and I watched some men with bows and
arrows preparing for a hunt. I felt the masculinity of the
place, the male initiations that had occurred at the very
spot where I sat. We talked about our lives, about their
confidence in me, and about the context of my visit with
them. I wanted to help them sell bananas in Rio, to end
the sarna, to aid them in becoming self-sufficient financially, and to bring two Xavante to teach tribal ways in
the United States. They would have a feast and dances
for twenty-four hours to pass a sacred knowledge on to
me.

I had to leave before the feast began, but, like a pitch-
er receiving fresh spring water, I watched as their wisdom was passed to me. For days I was like a computer
downloading centuries of tradition. I could barely sit up
as my body felt waves of water pouring over me, telling
my soul to be still and receive the gift. I returned to Rio
exhausted and changed. My world was over. I had
crossed the river.

My dreams were now of my own family back home
and the river of death—the deaths of my sister and later
my father. They would cross the river too. I wanted to be

near my father before he crossed over. Tserete had given me back a hidden strength to accept responsibility and authority. He led me safely through the cultural crossing. Now I was prepared to face the family crossing.

CHAPTER 2

Death in the Family

"Daddy's in Sarasota Memorial Hospital and doesn't look well. The cancer has moved to his liver, and he might not make it." My mother affectionately called my father "daddy" and he called her "mommy." She stayed by his side, sleeping in his private room at the hospital, hoping he would not leave his body until after he saw his grandchildren again.

I heard my mother's words and flew to Florida. "His skin has turned yellow. He has jaundice and he's lost a lot of weight," my mother explained on my arrival at the airport. "Don't be alarmed by his appearance. He's suffering and is not well."

When I saw my father sleeping from the drugs and painkillers and saw his orange milky-yellow skin, I could feel his terrible pain and knew he was ready to leave. When my mother left the room, he roused himself from his sleep, turned to me and said, "I saw the Virgin Mary. I saw her face. . . ." He had not recognized me yet; he was still dreaming of Her. I told him, "It's all right, she's coming for you, to take you home; I understand." Then I started to cry.

My father had never spoken of such things. He had never once had a vision of the Virgin, or at least had never told me. Now he had a glow about him—the shining when you are more outside the body than in it. In his terrible anguish, he looked stripped, only speaking from the heart with pure, unadulterated feeling.

"Foster, I've so little faith. I'm afraid to die. I want to see my grandchildren in New York. I don't have your faith." My father was a retired neuro-psychiatrist, the director of psychiatry at a prominent hospital, a man of science, a doctor listed in the annals of *Who's Who*. He had created one of the first psychiatric departments in a general hospital, and was a brilliant innovator who loved his work and helped the mentally ill. He went to church every Sunday, a devout Catholic, long after his children stopped attending Mass. Then, he felt his faith slipping.

"I don't know if I believe in an afterlife," he said.

When he was fully conscious and coherent, I told him, "I've got enough faith for both of us. I definitively know that there's an afterlife. I know there's a Creator. Daddy, when you're ready, you'll meet the Virgin Mary. You're going to a better place, and you'll realize your faith in a spiritual life. But I'm going to miss you."

My mother now stepped back into the room. She knew his time was limited. "The biopsies are too painful, too much pain," he said to us. The doctor needed to know what course of treatment to follow, but the biopsy needle was too large and hurt my father's liver. The doctor wanted to take a third biopsy, since the first two had yielded only dead tissue.

I told my father, "No more biopsies." Then I placed my hands, for the first time, on my father's physical body to strengthen his etheric body, the source of true healing. I had never physically worked on him, only from a distance through prayer and intention.

"Daddy, is it all right if I touch your body and perform an act of spiritual healing? I'm not promising miracles, but I need your permission, willingness, and faith." He nodded his head in exhaustion.

Compassion is the only word for what happened next. I never loved my father as much as in that moment. I started to listen to the organs of his body, to listen to his etheric sheath, the supersensible self, and I talked with my father's spirit. All I could do was calm him down and touch him in the most loving way I knew. He closed his eyes, and I could feel him sensing every gesture and movement of my hand. He followed me with an awareness which brought consciousness to the wounds. My gift is to see and listen in a clairvoyant way.

I touched every part of his body, shooting a clear sound from my vocal chords into his tissues, and moving light like an X-ray machine through each visualized organ containing the cancer.

My mother became uncomfortable and asked to leave the room. My actions seemed too bizarre for her, as were the strange songs, old shamanic songs streaming out of my mouth in harmonies. She was unprepared, a little afraid of what I might do. I am not superstitious like her. I was adding my own life force to my father's in a very spiritually scientific way.

What I felt was his Sun body, the solar body, next his Moon body, and then his Saturn body. That might sound strange but it is a preparation for death, returning him to his original state. Through his etheric body, I could see his past, what led to this moment, in an objective reading of the Akashic Record; and then I saw that his soul was about to collapse and give all its energy and memories to his astral body before he became spirit again. I wanted him to be free, free of the needless suffering that prolonging his stay on Earth would cause.

Finally, I worked on his Earth body, his material substance, the container we create with the Creator. I know we were created from the Sun, Moon, Saturn, and Earth—indeed from all of the cosmos—and that we are being prepared for our true spiritual bodies through our experience here.

My father was a truly individuated man. He developed his intellect, his intelligence, to a vast degree, and since 1992 he was miraculously in his heart. He had cancer for seven years: first non-Hodgkin's lymphoma, then Hodgkin's lymphoma, which moved from the neck to the liver, then circulated throughout his body, ravaging him. Yet, in this Sarasota hospital, he was transparent, glowing, somewhere far away. I met my father's soul in its humble naked form.

That is the second greatest gift a father can give his son: the sharing of his soul. The first is conception. This gift was not lost on me, the gift of mutual connection, of honor, of the incredible bonds that link father to son. Nothing was lost on me in that moment. He passed on his love, admiration, and respect for me. All I could do was touch him the way his soul had always touched mine.

My mother had to change his bedpans. Often he could not make it to the bathroom. She had once driven him through snowstorms to the hospital. And then she had found an energy, a fierceness to take care of his every need in his final years. She was boundless in her respect for him, and became strong in the process.

A life-threatening illness can have this sudden effect on people. We have boundless energy when we care for others, when we give selflessly because the situation urgently demands it. There is no choice in that love. We help, we suffer when they cannot sleep, and we see their ups and downs, the humility of it all.

I saw my mother change doing her duty to her husband. She worried more about him and less about herself. She began to love her children and grandchildren more because life now seemed finite, shorter than she had ever imagined. Life was, and is, precious. I felt that when my mother cried sitting next to my father—a swelling of emotion welled up in my throat like a lump, and I was awash in feeling. I was proud of my mother's undying love and care for him. It was a sign of the noble soul.

That care is the true test of a person's integrity. It reverses years of personal suffering and karma. It is the essence of what the Buddhists call *dharma*: service, compassion. I felt a tangible compassion and respect for my mother through her willingness to fight for his life in that small hospital room.

The nurses walked in on my display of Therapeutic Touch. They sat and watched while I explained how Therapeutic Touch was created by Dolores Krieger as a tool for nurses and lay people. They watched me identify cold spots in my father's auric field and see where to place the hands at the most blocked area. I explained the different color spectrums, and how they represent energy one could send through the body in a focused, directed way. We used a deep violet-blue light to aid my father's process of healing. They asked me to teach this method to the other nurses and aides on the floor. Interestingly enough, they had just recently requested from the hospital a course in Touch-for-Health. This was not coincidence. My father was in the right hands, with the most loving nurses I had ever met.

In my entire life, I had never been given so much respect from people working in a hospital. These particular nurses were thoughtful, intelligent, and open to new forms of self-healing and the healing of the mind and body. My respect for the hospital and its staff grew, and my heart opened in the cancer ward amidst the dying.

My father turned to the nurses and declared, "My son is a famous healer. He teaches people all over the world about true healing. He writes books and gives lectures instructing them in ways that improve their lives." I was amazed. He had never acknowledged my healing work to my face. After graduating from Georgetown University, I had always thought that he judged my choice of profession as a disappointment. I thought he wanted me to be a medical doctor like he was. Perhaps we were more alike than I had imagined. I never knew how much he respected and cared for my soul's work. Nothing was the same between us after that. I had to walk slowly to the rest room, where I wept for my father's acceptance of my true soul.

A warmth from the heart exuded from me, directed to the nurses, to total strangers walking the aisles of the hospital. I felt the soft-spoken compassion of the doctors and knew the long hours the staff endured while facing life-threatening illnesses. I saw how they often could not control their own tears after someone died surrounded by loved ones. My admiration grew for them and for their service. I felt how all of us are linked, how as a species we are reaching consciousness together, ending a deep sleep. I found the Christ in everyone, in people's smiles, even in drawn faces. I could feel intense loneliness in most of the rooms, where people felt abandoned to their body's destruction. I wanted to reach out to them, to tell them a total stranger cared, that there is a bigger picture. I wanted to look into each person's Akashic Record: all their accumulated memories stored in the body. I wanted to say just the right thing to free them and give them detachment. I knew on that incredible day that hospitals would call for my healing services in the future, like they had called my father, and that my work would lead me there. I knew that this was part of my personal calling to love.

My mother was engrossed in helping my father. She wanted me to complete with him. I finally asked him, "Daddy, are there any incompletions between us? I forgive you for everything in the past. I have no anger toward you, only a tremendous love that never ceases even when I pretend it's gone. I've never stopped loving you, Daddy, and I don't hold you accountable for any harm or wounding in the past. I see now you were the perfect father for me, and you did nothing wrong. Daddy, is there anything you need to let go of? Is there anything in the past you need to forgive me for?"

He said, "I've got only one regret. That I didn't live

longer and couldn't be there for you and your brother and sisters. I'm too young to die. I'm too young to die!"

"Daddy, it's all right to leave."

"But I want to see my grandchildren. I want to see them again in New York, to be strong enough to take the flight."

"I see three to four months of life left, and then it's time to go to the light. Ask your family to take the flights and see you while there's still time. Please, ask them to come. Don't be ashamed of your appearance in the hospital." He nodded his head in acceptance and reached over and took my hand. "When it's time to die, leave from your heart through the top of the head. You'll still remember your life. Your etheric body keeps all the memories. First, you'll review your life, and this could take a long time. You'll reexperience what you've done to others and you'll feel the effect of every action on them. You'll experience empathy and know the effect of every action on the world. When this is complete, you'll continue to learn in a kind of spiritual university. Like all the dead, you'll still be inside the realm of human beings, just as we're inside the realm of plants.

"You'll be like floating mind, floating intelligence. Go to the light, the warmth. Call for my sister Pat and let her help you to cross over to the city of intense light. See your spiritual self, what you're attaining here on Earth. You'll see your true essence and know that my own spiritual development in this life helps you. And learning your lessons on the other side helps me on Earth. I love you, Daddy. I hope that wasn't too much. I'm human, I'm going to miss you so much. You're going to a better place of nurturing. Don't be afraid. Leave when it's time."

"Foster, there's too much pain, I can't breathe. I can't stand the sharp pain, the suffering. Sometimes I can't move. It's too much for your mother to take care of me. She can't sleep at night. What'll she do without me to take care of her? Take care of her Foster, after I die."

I whispered in his ear, "When you die there's no pain. It's the cessation of suffering. It's freedom. I'm all right. I can take care of myself. I'm strong, self-sufficient now. So are Gerry, Fred, Yvonne, and your grandchildren. They're disciplined and stronger than we are at times. We'll all take care of Mother in her grief and mourning. Everyone will be O.K. You can go when you want to. I see three or four months. Live as if it's the last day. I love you. I'll always help you, in life or in death. I can perhaps help you when you cross over when the time is right."

"I don't want to suffer anymore. I love you all too much. I love you, Foster, and I never told you that."

You wait, as a son, all your life for those three words. "I love you." I knew he meant it because he does not use words freely. "I always will love you, Daddy. Memories live on beyond death. I will always remember the depth of our time together. You taught me so many things. I'm so grateful you created me with your love."

I keep his picture on a table top in my house with photographs of all my relatives—my great-grandfather, the Ypsilantis family, the Perrys from India and Australia, his mother, sister, my mother's father, mother, and my sister Anastasia and my other siblings. It is an altar with three candles for my ancestors. I know they assist me on the other side. I know I can only assist them through my conscious awareness, my spiritual life here.

When my mother left me at the airport to say goodbye after my brief visit with my father, I told her, "You
don't have to wait with me at the airport. He needs you
and you need to rest. I'm old enough now. I feel very
strong inside and mature. I've grown up. I can finally take
care of myself." My mother understood. She needed to be
near him in the final moments of his life. For me, that was
a moment of profound trust, a letting go of her obliga-
tions to me as her son. Something passed between mother and son, a respect, a maturing in our relationship. I
really could honestly take care of myself.

My father died a few days before his birthday, April
22. His funeral was scheduled for his birthday. He finally gave up to enter the next adventure.

My father's funeral was in the same Catholic church
that I attended as a child. I had not returned to St.
Aiden's church in Williston Park since I was a young, fid-
geting adolescent sitting next to my father at Sunday
mass. And I had never been a pallbearer, in the front line
of a funeral procession. The coffin was heavy with flowers, roses. I have never felt such a great sense of honor
as on that day. I felt a respect for the ritual. My father's
close friend spoke about him in the benediction, and I
saw my father's youth for the first time through his eyes.
There was so much that I never knew about him. I cried
profusely upon hearing this man's expression of love for
my father. I will never forget his kind words of bravery
and acknowledgment.

I love it when people are at their best, not brilliant,
but sincere in a blatantly honest way. That is what I saw

in my father's friend as he gave the benediction. Even the priest had a transcendent moment and spoke from his heart. He knew death and was not faking his sincerity. He spoke of impermanence and the desire to incarnate and nourish a family.

It was Easter time, and at his burial there were hundreds of Easter lilies. I felt Easter was his rebirth to a new kind of life. When they finished the burial prayers and everyone left the crypt, I stayed behind and sang an old East Indian chant—my father was part Indian by blood—the passing-over song of a great spirit, a great soul. I felt the rain of tears purifying the song as my one voice broke into several. The cracking voice, as it reached its epiphany, was the Logos of the universe singing through the apostles at Pentecost. My sister, who had died a year earlier, called herself a Pentecostal because she would feel the Logos come into her larynx and give birth to the joyful song of angels.

My mother watched me from a distance, and when I left his crypt, she came up to me and said, "You sang old Indian songs to your father. He would've liked that." She had never in her life acknowledged me in such a deep manner. I was so very honored to be her son at that moment. Those songs were my final tears of praise and grief.

Acceptance, nonjudgment had finally come, and I realized the depth of family love. I said to my father's spirit at his wake, "Father, forgive me, but I need to ask you for a favor from the other side. I have everything I've ever wanted, and I'm grateful for my health, but Father, I need a companion, a lover, someone who loves everything I am."

In three days, he answered my prayer, and I have loved that person in a deep, meaningful way ever since. My father found a perfect companion for me, and I have never felt alone since that day. That was his final gift to me.

In retrospect, I now see that Tserete of the Xavante was a kind of spiritual father to me. He gave me the courage to love and face my biological father at his death. They were my two fathers and guardians to maturity.

After my father's death, I perceived Chiron working behind these events. Although I would not become a medical doctor like my father, Chiron was preparing me for a deep form of shamanism, an inward medicine to heal the split between instinctual and spiritual life.

There is one version of the Chiron story in Greek myth in which he finds a cure for his wound from a plant—later named "centaury" after him. I wanted to return to the jungle to find that plant. I wanted to hear its spirit sing.

I left Sarasota, Florida for the Amazon of Brazil. I was visibly shaken, changed, grieving, yet free to cultivate the soul of the inner father.

PART TWO

THE *Violet* *Forest*
AND
THE *Violet* *Bardo*

CHAPTER 3

Paje, Safeguard the World

The Amazon River basin contains the largest volume of fresh water in the world, draining nearly half of South America. From the Andes of Peru, where it is called the Alto Maranon, it flows 3400 miles to the coast of Brazil. I flew to different parts of the Amazon to gain a broader perspective of its great expanse. I was entranced by every place I visited, but it was south of the river that I felt a true kinship with the many tribes that live off its waters.

I kept my first visits to the rain forest south of the Amazon a secret from my friends. I feared their criticism of my new exploration of psychoactive plant substances with tribal people. I did not want colleagues to think that I was ingesting recreational drugs. I wanted to drink *mucuna* with a tribe and *ayahuasca* with a trained shaman. This was a serious quest to understand the strange otherworldly perceptions that exist in shamanic cultures. The knowledge and use of plants to alter one's state of mind are ancient tools to access humankind's cultural and religious archetypes. Robert Graves[1] has suggested that the centaurs in Greece became wild and unruly through ingesting *Amanita muscaria* mushrooms. These mushrooms, a common hallucinogen of great antiquity, are used to induce shamanic trance.

When I first entered the rain forest south of the Amazon, I felt my senses being overwhelmed—as if I were submerged in a hallucination in which the forest spoke directly to my soul. I began my journey with reverence and awe for the rituals and perceptions of native people. I was in awe of the immensity of Brazil and felt very small compared to the greatness of the natural world. I learned to respect nature in a whole new way and to release any greed for knowledge of inner dimensions. A new world opened its gates, and I had to find the poetry of the Amazon forest.

Night was descending when I arrived at the rain forest near Manaus, Brazil. Even before ingesting the sacred mucuna plant, I was already merging with the landscape. The openheartedness and patience of the Amazon, this timeless world of sultry heat, washed my soul in fevers and starless nights. I was moving toward forest, mist, and water—landscapes that hold the insoluble mystery of humankind.

I met men called *pajes*, or shamans, with all-seeing eyes, exuberantly humorous, indomitable and dauntless in their beliefs. I saw the onslaught of the modern world on a way of life based in ancient tradition. I was aware of the war inflicted on the indigenous people of Brazil, the silent battles. I saw the black surfaces of forests abandoned and burned. I saw the silence of a sea amidst this destruction.

Brazil is immense, expanding, while the indigenous peoples retreat into the interior. I want a world where the standard of living and the way of life are consonant with human dignity, where many tribes co-exist, linked by waterways and plains, traveling by canoe and foot to form a community and a nation. I trace my existence to the Amazon River, to its blood in my veins. The rain forest infuses its harmonious, scenic awareness into the soul. I meet humorous and perceptive people here, untainted by modern society. The subtle balance of human relationships, a natural order, fills the senses with honor. Here I understand the inner wisdom of mutual respect.

Rosy spoonbills and white egrets, exquisite birds, flew over my head when I arrived. All around me I heard the screech of parrots and monkeys; I sensed the presence of the fox and alligator, the yellow puma, the ants burrowing in the ground of the forest heat, the razor-toothed piranha—guardian of the waters—and fish swimming along the riverside for berries and fallen fruits. The winter brings the rains in mid-November, and the summer warms and dries the land in May with a cloudless expanse of blue. I followed the turtles to the river's edge. Hundreds of turtle eggs lay hidden in the banks of tributaries. I saw anteaters emerge from the forest, foraging for food.

I felt the dances of shamans on leaves, heard the high-pitched cries of Indians mimicking birds, the spoken words of the lineage keepers echoing through the misty air. I stumbled across powerful, evocative waterfalls. These natives are part of nature, inhabiting the world of plants, flowers, waterfalls, and birds. They live in tribal unity where responsibilities are shared. Power is diluted for the benefit of all. No one needs to command. Dignity is more important than power.

The supernatural lays its blanket of peace over the forest—freedom without fear. Every child belongs to a community, not an individual parent. There is an open-ness, a collaboration of people. No one disturbed me while I sat in the immense forest at night. They passed by me in silence.

Young men were bathing in the river, half-hidden in the mist, as I approached. The water was warm, and they made a whooping sound with their voices. Other villagers had just finished fishing, and some had gathered manioc tubers. (The poisonous manioc root is scraped and washed until it is no longer toxic, then boiled to make the juice called *mandioca brava*, which is their food or to make body paint that is bright red. The manioc root is ground for making bread. It is the staple food of the forest.)

The men were cleaning themselves, grooming with a sense of moral purity. They bartered and exchanged and gossiped at night. Fish and manioc were eaten, the fish grilled sizzling on the open fire. I was reminded of a Xingu Indian shaman who, at such gatherings, intimate-ly called out the names of different spirits. He would shout, "Yanama, Kaurate, Kalaramane." He chanted also to the Moon and kept the air lively with song. Pajes do not want anyone's soul stolen. That is why they sing so fully, so loudly, to keep the spirits dancing and happy. No soul thefts happen while the pajes chant. But I have heard stories of apparitions here. An old man is often seen on the riverbanks with long, flowing white hair and with a halo around his head.

An Indian is said to have three souls: two that are finite, created at conception and leaving at death, and one that is eternal essence and the source of beauty and honor. For them, death is a gateway to another life on a river without fish, dancing with the Moon and with the weaving pictures of the ether—the currents of eternity. At death some souls battle the birds like Guardians of the Threshold. The birds violently war against the journeying souls, mercilessly judging people at the door of death. If the initiates defeat their bird counterparts through seeing their own inner war with the astral—their disruptive karmic nature—in the bird's behavior and survive being eaten, they will live on in eternity with the wings of that bird, undisturbed in the heavens. The initiates will be reborn on the other side of the gate as new beings in a new spiritual village.

I have often sat at night in the forest, in the sacred dome of Earth, where the land regains its energy. Pajes sing and safeguard this world we live in and make me grateful to be alive. I care for this place and the daily round and rhythm of creation. Songs of the Logos come and go, bringing order to the universe. There is a natural harmony between the spirit and the conditions of life. I am hopeful, despite the imperfections of the everyday world, feeling my spirit challenged, supported, and encouraged.

No river belongs to a person, but we are borne on its silent tide—the passing hours—near the garlands of wild vine. I have felt the abundance of fruit, the goddess of plenty, the generous earth. I have seen men wrestling with vigor and courage, circling each other, slapping and trying to throw one another off balance with no shame. Here I have known warriors undefeated in battle, but I have never seen a warrior humiliated in defeat.

A jaguar, yellow with black spots, once showed itself to me in the forest, running past me as an omen, as a sign. It was chasing its prey. My power animals are both predators and prey, and I am wary of a person who has only predators for power animals. A Brazilian man named Pirai, who lived with many tribes in the north and wrote down their languages in dictionaries, told me that his power animal was an earthworm. Dawn Eagle Woman, my close friend, remarked to him, "Pirai, you will win in the end, my friend." The worms devour the remains of organic life and do win in the end. Pirai also told us how he wandered through the jungle for weeks eating only a specific root—one that was good for the ovaries—in order to survive. Unfortunately, the root did him no good since he had no ovaries! The humor of the Amazon people is contagious.

I am reminiscing, remembering all my visits to Brazil, to its tribes, its vast expanses of savannah and forest. My life changed there. I became more of an "I," more self-conscious, and more free to be in the spirit of greatness. I was no longer part of a tribe, no longer in a community of souls; my individuality became my destiny. We have to awaken from the dream of collectivity, the dream of the group soul.

CHAPTER 4

The Color Violet:
Entrance into the Bardo

On this my second visit to the rain forest near Manaus, I prayed on the trip in, emptied, purifying my mind to enter the old forest. Night was descending when I arrived, and the forest was filled with sounds of birds. At one point, I could vaguely see an anaconda snake moving past me along a fallen hollow tree. The next morning I would discover an anaconda's skin. I was shedding my own skin in the twilight. The stillness was a kind of echo. A blackness encroached on the light, and I was surrounded by a void.

My Brazilian friends were now asleep in camp after our long hike. I was alone in the vast thickness of moist air. I was on an odyssey into the heart of Brazil. I remembered a phrase from the Greek poet Homer, the "wine dark sea." I had consciously immersed myself in that sea.

Homer was said to be blind. When you close your eyes and can see little ambient light, rhodopsin, a pigment of the rods of your eyes, gives darkness a deep-violet color. Sitting in meditation or simply closing my eyes, I was submerged in darkness but could still see. Theodore Roethke wrote, "In a dark time the eyes begin to see."[1]

In the Violet Forest, I saw the color of wine everywhere. What did I experience in my mother's womb?

There is fetal touch, a warmth of sensation, weightlessness without a fixed notion of place. This is the general description of the inner worlds—the encounter with the Great Mother, the flow of aliment within her body. It also accounts for the concentration later in life on the navel area. Inner and outer distinctions dissolve in the womb.

When we close the ears, mouth, nose, eyes, we are reentering the womb for the second birth, the spiritual birth. The first birth is by water, and the second, as John the Baptist demonstrated, is by spirit. It is warm, nurturing, the essence of feeling.

That night I could feel my whole body turning violet in the Amazon. The forest surrounded me like a fortress. The fire bugs whirled about like glowing dust, blinking on and off in the sweltering heat. The air acted as an envelope of protection. I was becoming incandescent from within. I could no longer perceive the past or future with my senses heightened. There was no place to go or hide. I was in the unknown, unafraid. The trees swayed, rhythmically rocking. I was caught in a moment of real time.

I understood meditation at that moment: the willingness to close down the senses, the body listening only to internal sounds. I could hear my eardrum clapping, the blood moving through my veins. The jungle turned my body inside out. I journeyed into the womb of darkness.

Surrendering to the Amazon, I could meditate for the first time as a witness, observing fleeting thoughts and opening my etheric body to a greater consciousness—the world beyond the veils. I was small in its immensity and more awake than the animals.

No sleep came that night. I stood erect like a tree, my

spine like an inner tree. The forest growing within told me, "Focus your heart on one point and nothing is impossible." I heard its words preparing me for the next step.

"God is experience itself. God partakes in all experience. God is all we live and breathe. If you become the soul of the mind, you are at rest in it and you rest in the mystic sea, in the wine dark sea." We are all blind like Homer, but can still see this violet wine. "In the stillness of the heart," the forest said, "is the awakening of the breath."

The Greek word for violet is *ion*; it describes both red and deep blue. The Greek nobles wore violet. Athens was called the violet-crowned city. In Rome, only Caesars wore the color purple. In Catholicism, purple is second only to white. The Pope wears a purple cap. It is the color of exultation, of transmutation and freedom.

Shamanism, for me, is a violet sea. The shaman is a god-man, a mythopoet. Shamanism is the experience of ecstatic living. It has deep roots throughout the world and could very well be the foundation of the Judeo-Christian tradition, of Tibetan Buddhism (through the Bon Po tradition), and of the Vedic Era in India (circa 1000 B.C.). It is the practice of inducing cosmic memory—with or without trance.

Intentionally induced trances produce ecstatic un-ion with the divine and are the core basis of ancient shamanism. Elder practitioners of this art created from their experience of the spirit world the foundation of yoga, which means "union" or to "yoke together" with God, or in India, Brahman.

Shaman are not priests, but mentors, companions, friends on the journey to true clairvoyance. Their special knowledge is of the unseen world. They can empty their minds and go into trances or remain conscious in the etheric worlds once they have passed the Guardians of Death. Shamans primarily use myths, fairy tales, to describe experiences of trance states in veiled ways. They pass on their knowledge through rites of passage at puberty. Shamans often give young men poisonous plants to eat while on a "vision quest" in the forest. If a boy survives and returns to the village, he is welcomed into the community as a man with a role. That was my "rite of passage" in Brazil, drinking the mucuna as a tonic for my vision quest.

Shamans remember the past through the ancestors and through direct experience of their etheric bodies or from the Akashic Records, a direct line to the past and future. Shamans use their breathing and certain body postures to see beyond time. This is one of the primary goals of the vision quest.

The word spiritual derives from the Latin word for breath. Breath is spirit. God is experience and awareness in the breath. Dolphins are common teachers of shamans by willfully, easily, stopping their breathing for long periods of time. Delphi in Greece means "place of the dolphin." In yoga, it is the cycle of inhalation and exhalation that is the wheel of birth and death.

According to Patanjali, in the Yoga Sutras, breath can be controlled for *kaivalya* or liberation. *Kumbhaka*, a phenomenon known to yogis, is when the lungs fill with air and trance states occur. Breath is felt in the sinuses, and held between the eyebrows in the shape of a bird's wing span. This is the description of the frontal suture of the brow (the suture is the point of an embryonic division in the frontal lobe). When breath enters the sinuses, *prana* or oxygen enters the cranium. The breath opens the gate of the skull.

The Hindus understand these fundamental techniques when they mark the forehead with a starlike *tilak* or by three vertical lines where the breath enters the skull. This point is the gate of Brahman. Breath enters the heart, pelvis, legs, head, and the whole body (called *vyana*). The yogi concentrates on the root of breathing located in the etheric body at the pituitary gland.

When the yogi concentrates on the pituitary, a hormone is released that awakens the pineal gland. Its awakening is a shattering experience for the unprepared. The release of the pituitary hormone causes a tearing of consciousness and can be very dangerous for the uninitiated. It can lead to epilepsy. A shaman learns to cleanse and purify the emotions and body through fasting, right thought, mindfulness, contemplation, and meditation on the chakras or lotuses, so as to balance the hormone levels of testosterone, adrenaline, and thyroxine, which can interfere with the pituitary hormone. The pituitary gland controls the body and initiates spiritual awakening through this hormone.

We can activate this process through controlled respiration, slowing down the heart and lungs, stilling the mind, and then gazing at the root in the forehead: the pituitary. We enter the breath and a crack opens into the pineal like a rush of energy, like lightning. There is a flash and beyond that light is *samadhi*, an ending of karma.

The whole process is the root of initiation passed down over many generations. This experience is now happening to thousands of people as a result of grace and evolution. My intention is to help people understand this process through my experience of the pituitary awakening. We must be prepared to face the shadow, the rejected self, and to enter the other worlds with patience, concentration, and spiritual cognition so as to become conscious adepts. My last thought, while taking the poisonous mucuna sap on my vision quest, was of the Eleusinian Mysteries of Greece and how initiation is a preparation for dying. What would it be like to not-do, to extinguish the senses? What exists beyond the senses? I know that karma is created through the consequences of actions and suffering by afflictions which create conditioned responses in the nervous system. By repetitive breathing, yogis clear their nervous systems. I wanted to find a middle way beyond the old Hindu path for perceiving the etheric worlds.

The term *bardo* denotes transition, any transition. The bardo states are described in *The Tibetan Book of the Dead* as the layers of transition to a new life at death. I was determined to experience the bardo of death while alive. I entered into a violet adventure through my personal patterns of darkness and the psychological and karmic complexes of the psyche. With this aim, I called in a cascade of experiences that shook me. What followed was the violet bardo. To transmute my awareness, I went on a rollercoaster ride of seduction, obsession, numbness, and passion to reach the final bardo of freedom. I ingested many diverse plant substances from 1993 to 1996 and recorded these experiences in my journals. These plants initiated me, making me face my own pain and the power of seduction and sacrifice, leading to a new understanding of discernment. The personal stories of the violet bardo are never flattering, but they are the true telling of how I moved from the love of power to the power to love.

CHAPTER 5

Seduction and Ayahuasca

Webster's Dictionary defines the verb to seduce as *se-*, "apart" and *ducere*, "to lead"[1], i.e, to lead apart. A friend told me, "Since Pluto is leaving Scorpio and moving into Sagittarius, the old patterns of seduction are leaving. This is a strong lesson to understand after the death of your father. It is the one hindrance to real love." From experience, I knew she was right.

Many teachers or authorities—facilitators—can easily sabotage themselves through seduction. Accounts of therapists or spiritual teachers seducing their clients or devotees are innumerable, pointing to the intoxication of power. A large number of Catholic priests have also come under scrutiny for sexual misconduct. This is a form of self-sabotage which destroys the fragility of love instead of creating bonds of intimacy. Seduction is often motivated by a desperate need to be loved.

I wanted people to love me, and that need for admiration began to destroy my work. In healing work, one's sexual energy needs to be transmuted, not used to entice people through personal charisma or to manipulate an audience. Instead of bringing a group into harmony, unconscious sexual energy splits them apart. This need to be loved and accepted by an adoring audience can lead to obsessive behavior for both the teacher and the student.

Patterns of seduction are unconscious for the most part. After the publication of my first book, I received numerous calls from women asking me how tall I was, the color of my hair, and if I was still single? A number of women after a workshop in Brazil wrote letters to me declaring that I was their "soul mate" and why didn't I realize it? Some women wanted me all to themselves and tried to draw me away from Dawn Eagle Woman, my partner in work. Many women declared that they did workshops with me because I was their "twin flame."

Eventually I realized that I was creating this behavior, that my sexual energy was unconsciously seducing people, hooking them with projections of being the ideal mate. I needed to create the intention to be clean in my work, and to vigilantly release the need to seduce people for love or attention. Once I identified how seduction undermined the real essence of my soul and work and how it gave me a surrogate love and an audience in total projection, I began to stop it.

I dreamed of orgies in ancient Greece, recalled the pain of rejection in relationships and the avoidance of that pain. I remembered how my father, who had an office in our home, had women in therapy who would become obsessed with him and eventually turn violent. One woman beeped her horn outside our front door and when my father stepped outside to talk to her, she pulled a gun on him. The police had to talk her into surrendering her weapon and going to the hospital. Another woman entered our house yelling about our dogs and how they were after her and going on about her obsession with my father. I would often answer the phone, and women would be calling for my father, telling me they would commit suicide if they couldn't speak to him at that very moment.

After my father's death, I encountered this unconscious projection of the savior/lover/father. I received women's projections of the perfect sensitive mate, handsome and heart-oriented. I realized that I was leaking the seducer archetype, and I searched my soul to find and close the opening. I wanted to release the confused energy that I picked up as a child being exposed to my father's obsessive clients. I wondered what was in his being that attracted those particular experiences to him.

In all my next workshops, I began to announce my seduction pattern of needing to be liked and how it undermined me. Then I moved the energy of seduction up my spine and became a teacher in a clean way. I could actually turn to teaching in depth and not try to satisfy all the needs of my audience. I could see how audiences had become mother figures, and I was the child burdened with their/her repressed sexuality. Like a child, I was still trying to satisfy my mother's sexual needs. Like my father, I was trying to satisfy my client's emotional needs. I had lost the role as the facilitator and began to engage people on a co-dependent level. I wanted the audience to fulfill some need in me, and instead of bringing love, it brought on more seduction and feelings of betrayal.

My pattern of seduction finally became fully conscious to me in Peru. After my father's death, I needed to mourn and to release him, but I needed an even longer time to grieve his loss. Grief fills a man, a son, and I was grieving the past, the old life. I felt I had to become a father, a responsible man. I started to think about insurance, IRAs, mutual funds, security, raising a family. Yet the grieving was cut short, and I began losing myself in denial through business.

I was scheduled to lead a tour to sacred sites in Peru. For three years, I had been leading shamanic voyages to the Peruvian Amazon and had visited remote inland tribes. I had been introduced to ayahuasca by a Peruvian shaman. This particular ayahuascero had his own recipe of combining the vine (which is the basis of ayahuasca) with the leaf of the chicha plant. I learned how the combination helped activate a kind of mescaline for deeper shamanic work.

Chanting is an integral part of the ceremony of taking ayahuasca, and these sacred songs called *icaros* play a transformative role. For the true ayahuasca experience, one needs to hear a succession of icaros sung by shamans throughout the ceremony. These songs are generations old, taught by elders to apprentices. Some icaros are learned directly from spirits encountered during the ayahuasca ceremony. Each icaro calls in a specific spirit or cast of spirits who acts as a vehicle to other worlds, times, and dimensions.

I have encountered songs of buildings where I was instantly transported to Incan temples. I have heard boat songs, jaguar songs, and songs of the anaconda snake. Each time a healing or environment was created for contact with other dimensions of the rain forest. Many participants in these pioneering expeditions would experience similar events but from different viewpoints.

The icaros stabilize and guide the journeys of the plant. Otherwise, taking ayahuasca can be dangerous, wild, whirling, and an often frightening adventure for the unprepared.

Ayahuasca, as it is called in the Quechua tongue, is taken to be able to see into the spirit world. It is vision-inducing, coming from the psychoactive vine called *Anisteriopsis*, which is then mixed with another plant. The drink is used by shamans to identify the causes of illnesses and to heal through the aid of the plant. Recently, there has been a renaissance surrounding psychoactive substances by anthropologists, ethnobotanists, and spiritual explorers entering the jungles of Ecuador, Peru, and Brazil. For instance, Brazil has two distinct ayahuasca religions, called Santo Daime and Unaio de Vegetal, which have large followings and foreign members. Many Westerners are now undergoing long-term apprenticeships with this plant substance. Curiosity brought me to the plant and to Peru.

First, we begin the ceremony at night, and the whole town remains silent, knowing what is about to take place. Sight and hearing are acute during the entire journey. Under the drink's influence, participants have heard sounds from a mile away and even farther distances in the jungle. I usually drink only a third of a cup. Others in the group will drink up to three-and-a-half cups. After drinking, the shamans begin to work on specific persons through singing the icaros and blowing tobacco smoke over the pituitary and pineal glands and praying. They will also suck out spirits from our bodies with breath work. With our eyes closed or open, multicolored visions of extraordinary clarity and bizarre opalescence begin with iridescent colors such as lime green, shocking pink, and silver. Geometric patterns form at the edges of most visions and continually repeat and merge into one another. The effect is like a rushing river of images—like a kaleidoscope depicting animals of the jungle, religious symbols from many traditions, and fantastic landscapes in other worlds.

It was on ayahuasca that I realized just how pure my body was. Less than a third of a cup lasted me for seventeen hours of visions, which began within fifteen minutes after drinking. I also discovered that I did not need the ayahuasca to see clairvoyantly. This plant is for those who have not done intensive yoga and tantric work. It is a boost for those who do not see easily. In my everyday consciousness, I do not feel dense, so ayahuasca was too strong, too potent for me. It literally screams images at you.

On one occasion, the plant immediately talked to me through a form of telepathy. Its spirit, which is both female and male, explained how I had used the plant in other lives and that I had been with many of my current apprentices in those lives. The plant then introduced me to these people in the course of the journey. Next the plant itself tried to seduce me to show my own seduction patterns. First the plant was a woman and when that did not work, she tried to seduce me as a man. Like truth serum, the plant substance began to show me just how sexual I had become. The plant woman was a vine with a scent and a huge aura of love. She surrounded me, reminding me that I do not have to be everything for everyone. She told me that, if I had sex with her, I would become an ayahuascero. I told her that no one can make me do anything against my will.

The plant showed the fragility of my personality, and how it is still fairly immature in its ego development. She said the age of Kali Yuga has ended and that we are in the midst of a spiritual awakening of our entire species through the heart development of the personality and ego. She felt I needed to develop a strong sense of identity, and that the ego was supportive as long as I knew its limitations. She told me to become a solar being through the reflected light of the emotional, lunar nature. Then I was shown the phases of the Moon and their effect on the dragon currents of Earth. She revealed the inner workings of the emotional body as phases of the Mother.

She told me that my supersensible self was emerging as a hybrid soul incorporating the conscious personality in the world and the greater self. It was all a training in perception. Did I want to release my need to be seduced in order to go further on the path of the true integrated self?

I mentally spoke to her and released it. She said I had met, through my father's intervention, a person that I would love for life. She said it would be an Aquarian relationship, a new equality in reciprocated love and that we would support each other's independence of spirit, and I would learn to break the cords of insecurity between us. In love I had to learn to be independent and self-reliant emotionally. She showed me how infatuation created cords of dependency to lovers and that I had to be aware of my insecurity around rejection. In order to break the emotional cords that drain me, sucking out the life force, I must not abandon my soul and identity in love.

Then, I had a revelation on ayahuasca. I began to feel that the fate of the Earth was intricately connected to the Moon cycles. The plant showed me how the lunar cycle specifically affected the evolution of mammals, reptiles, and birds. The human being was conceived first, before the plants and animals, in a divine image, an etheric body, not a physical one. We would therefore be the last to evolve. We were still not solid when the reptiles, other mammals, and birds were coming into form. We were like a constantly changing weather pattern of emotional states. The astral body or emotional body was forming at that time through feeling and sensations. During the Paleozoic and Mesozoic eras, the etheric bodies of humans were forming as patterns from the Moon. We were being created from the ethers and only later became flesh, bone, and blood. The blood holds the memory of the etheric blueprint of our becoming.

I saw how the astral or emotional bodies filled our physical bodies as a primordial dragon, a birdlike creature, or a mammal. I saw how this related to clan membership in tribes. The spine and lower brain are a remnant of the reptilian nature, the dragon. This is responsible for our instincts and subconscious impulses.

The dragon was also faced by Michael Harner in his groundbreaking book, *The Way of the Shaman*. He encountered a dragon who boasted that it was Lord of the World. In my own shamanic journey, I was not seduced by the dragon, but saw that Earth was my witness and that the Lord of Illusion would not control my destiny. I did not have to slay the dragon or overcome it but could make it an ally to see through illusion. I needed to learn to trust emotion, and to consciously work at harmonizing my emotions with the lunar cycle; this would cause a hormone to secrete into my pituitary gland. The ayahuasca plant said that the hummingbird was my guide to the nectar of the lunar elixir in the neuro-secretions of my brain.

I had to shake hands with the dragon. If I stopped seducing on an unconscious level, I would not be seduced by illusion—what Rudolf Steiner calls *Kamaloca*. I had to be flexible emotionally, be a warrior in spirit and discern my true Self, not just through dreams but with my eyes open.

The plant told me that I would face three tests to build up strength. The first was that a dark shaman had realized my light and would invade my body. I would need the help of a Hunting Lodge—a group of souls who would clear me of the dark dragon spirit—as a way to deal with malevolent spirits and entities. This is a time of the Reckoning when all of humanity's lies, withholds, secrets, and hypocrisies will be exposed. We, as a species, must now stop lying to ourselves about our values.

The second test would be for me to face my pattern of seduction in a clear way; it would come in the form of a woman who would play the temptress to help me to see it. She would be like the ayahuasca plant, would call herself the dragon, and disrupt my work, teaching a profound lesson in obsessive sexuality. She would do this as a gift for both of our awakenings.

The third test involved responsibility with finances, energy, teaching, and humility. Could I accept the maturity of being a teacher and remain balanced and not sabotage myself with seduction a third time? The seduction of money, religion, and sexuality—the main focus of external power—can be transformed into a quest for love and freedom by being who I really am—alone or with another in relationship.

This was a kind of shock therapy. Each time the ayahuascero sang the icaros, the plant released from my intestines a huge effluence of liquid to my heart and brain. More visions would come, bringing extensive traveling for seventeen hours. There was a marked decline in visions after the icaros ended, and a gradual coming down to Earth, like a slow slide.

The plant warned me that the dark shaman had entered my body because of my unfamiliarity with ayahuasca in this life. To protect myself sufficiently in this kind of out-of-body experience, I should have been more alert and vigilant. Also, the plant said that I had been seduced by this shaman in another life, and that I needed to end my own past-life cycle of seduction as a shaman with my patients. This was my "seduction karma."

Only when you leave your body for a moment can another person or spirit enter you. The dark shaman was now residing in me, and I felt him talk through my mouth. I learned to suppress him. Through active meditation, I tried to make him leave, but I clearly needed the support and help of other human beings. I had tried to protect my friends on the expedition while they were journeying on ayahuasca, and meanwhile I had left myself open to attack and possession.

Drained and exhausted from the plant substance, I slept for hours. I recovered almost immediately at the end of the next day with a strange vitality. Many people in the group I had brought to Peru experienced only sleep, while others had vivid images after ingesting the plant. We got together to discuss our journeys. Some recalled an insect metamorphosis for twelve to fifteen hours. A few experienced a catharsis through vomiting or seeing a buried memory of abuse in childhood. A few had lovely journeys of calm and peace with active adventures in color. None of us remained the same. I cannot recommend the ayahuasca experience. After much rumination, I decided to not pursue ayahuasca again. The three tests of the plant still awaited me.

At the Temple of the Moon, on the Island of the Moon in Lake Titicaca in what is now Bolivia, I witnessed a remarkable event. Our tour group was sitting in a circle while an Inca man chanted in gratitude, and I witnessed an Inca *despacho* ceremony. I saw, with my eyes open, the Moon falling out of the sky toward our circle, and shattering in a million particles of light over our bodies. I felt a kinship with the Moon.

The Moon would help heal my need to be loved inappropriately and help me to respect myself. In seduction, self-respect is lost and boundaries are strangely blurred. I wanted to help myself and others to see beyond their projection of me to the real love inside of them. I was only a mirror for their self-love. I thanked the ayahuasca plant, but told it that I would not be an apprentice. I was, in fact, too open, too sensitive, and it was not right for me. I was ready for a gradual awakening to enlightenment. My need for quick visions was over.

CHAPTER 6

San Pedro

Many students have asked why I explored ayahuasca, *sanango*, peyote, or the cactus called San Pedro, and I tell them that this was part of my training for a specific time in my life and that it brought benefit: I had to learn in a difficult way that it was not right for me. With psychoactive plants the process of spiritual development is speeded up with less time to digest the full, more subtle meanings of the journey. I was also too open and sensitive and could attain many states of consciousness without their help.

Ayahuasca is also known as *yaje*, *natema*, and *Daime*. It is most commonly made from the vine of *Baniteriopsis caapi* and the leaves of *Diploterys* species. It has been used for centuries in the Amazon and throughout South America. Contemporary shamans and curanderos still use ayahuasca in shamanic divination and healing ceremonies. The highly psychoactive DMT and other tryptamines found in the additive plants are what creates its effect.

I have only taken ayahuasca under the tutelage of experienced shamans in traditional settings. In Brazil, the Santo Daime ayahuasca "cult" has the hummingbird as one of its main symbols. My work has been to discover hummingbird medicine and its possible benefits. I also adhere to specific purification diets consisting of plantains, fish, and rice, prohibiting sugar, salt, spices, and meat. In addition I restrict sexual activity to specifically focus and enhance the experience.

In Peru I met a shaman named Augustine who introduced me to San Pedro—a cactus that produces a warm, somatic feeling in the body, a caring sense of peace and well-being, and occasional visions. It grows in Peru as well as many other locations in South and Central America and the southwestern United States. It is common, available, and gentle. Augustine was an alcoholic who met a shaman who used San Pedro, and he had his addiction dissolved in one sitting. He was duly impressed and now teaches about this cactus in specific ceremonies and helps many addicts quit drugs and alcohol.

In two separate groups in Peru over consecutive years, I worked with Augustine to observe the effects of San Pedro for healing. The first group of twenty people took the drink of the cactus in tea form. The shamans cultivate and pray with the cactus before picking and ingesting it. The whole cactus is ground up to form the tea. Our group was in Winay Wayna on the Inca Trail near Machu Picchu. We slept outdoors in sleeping bags to keep warm because of the initial chills in the body soon after ingestion.

The first cup was passed around, and prayers were said to the spirit of the plant to regulate and balance the experience. Everyone was quiet, meditative, and centered. I had memories of Eleusis in Greece and the cup of mead given to the initiates, as well as the gentleness of peyote tepee ceremonies when the songs are sung correctly for the uplifting of all. I understood the role of plant substances and even flower essences, tinctures, and elixirs. I wanted a grounded spirituality, an earth-based connection to the plant and animal kingdoms. Having studied the art of tracking animals and the proper use of gathering and cultivating herbs at specific Moon times, I then wanted to study plants and their role in healing and awakening spiritually with a clear focus and intention. Protection is essential.

In my first experience of San Pedro, I experienced chills, then full bodily warmth while walking into a Crystal Mountain cave near Winay Wayna. Upon entering I bowed before an altar and was initiated by the Guardian of the Threshold into clear seeing of light worlds. I also had a dynamic insight into bodywork, which I performed on others while under the influence. I never left my body as I had with ayahuasca, but stayed completely inside, feeling every sensation physically.

On ayahuasca, visions came with my eyes open or closed; on San Pedro, I could control the visions and open my eyes to stop them—except once, when I left the group to relieve myself. The shaman directed me to a secluded area of the ruin. I walked forward a few feet and saw a remarkable vision. Standing there was what I took to be a living kachina—a spirit from the San Francisco Peaks in Arizona that only descends for the Hopi, Zuni, and other Native American nations. I was face-to-face with an ancient spirit with huge upper-body muscles and short legs whose face kept changing like a hologram of many composite kachinas. He looked at the stars with affection and compassion, and I was detached yet fascinated by his serenity and beauty.

He was an ancient guardian, a true spirit being who turned around to look at me stoically. He also guarded Winay Wayna and was the gatekeeper for our group that evening. I could see him with my eyes open, fully aware, with the stars brilliantly shining around our heads. For thirty minutes, I watched him, remembering every detail of his shape, size, and masks. I grew to love his changing form and felt connected to his spirit in an indescribable way. He touched my soul and seemed so friendly, benign, and ancient. That we share this planet with so many spirit beings was an expansive clear-headed insight.

I then called over a woman in the group who claimed she was not having a heightened experience. She was restless and felt the San Pedro had no effect. I took her by the hand, saying I wanted her to see something. She walked to the outside area of the temple, where I had been standing, and said, "What? I don't see anything." I told her to focus her eyes to her right and see who was sitting on the rock. She almost fell over. Her eyes adjusted, and she began to cry. This was real for her. She was overwhelmed with compassion for this large, strange creature. The spirit looked at her and then looked away, contemplating the sky. She felt immediately connected to Peru and its mysteries and was changed forever. Afterward her depressions started to lift, and she began to feel rooted. She was also able to release her grief over her husband's death.

No statue of nature gods came close to what I experienced with her. The feeling was kinship with another sentient life form formerly invisible to my eyes. I thanked San Pedro for that gift and never have forgotten.

In my second experience of San Pedro, I was with another group who approached a cave, adorned with the imprint of a snake, in the Urubamba Valley of Peru. The shaman had us sit in a circle outside the entrance in broad daylight. As the San Pedro took effect, we each walked into the dark cave with eyes closed, following with one hand the imprinted relief of the snake on the cave wall. A man in our group, Andy, played the didgeridoo, and I sang to guide the experience. I was becoming familiar with the plant and its friendly, gentle way.

My first and only vision there was not of Peru but of Tibet. In it I was walking through the mountains to a cave bridge and was greeted by an old lama. He said that I have a name in Shamballah and that I was entering their retreat. I spent three hours in Shamballah gardening, meditating, doing research in the library, and talking to various people. I felt part of a family, a remembrance. The lama described a place in the Andes called Amara-mu-ru in the Valley of the Blue Moon, also called the Valley of the Seven Rays. He remarked that it had a similar purpose to Shamballah, and it was being prepared for when human beings become consciously aware of their nature and could see their solar essence. We spoke of Patanjali and the Yoga Sutras in depth, and I saw how the pineal gland in my body is a shrinking remnant of an organ that, in Atlantean times, was originally on top of the head and now has shrunk to a small pea-shaped gland in the center of the brain. He helped me to make it flexible, to loosen it from its encasement.

After I came back, I dreamt that night of entering the Inner Earth in four distinct locations. One was in Peru near a tribe a few hours hike from Iquitos. A large cave entrance actually did exist there. I was told in Iquitos about a man named Archimedes who had successfully navigated the blackness of the cave and met with the Inner Earth civilization; he brought back specific spiritual insights along with stones and crystals not seen on the surface of the planet.

I had heard that a Japanese television crew tried to film this particular portal in the Earth, but after one hour of walking in total darkness among the rats, spiders, and worms, they freaked out and one man committed suicide by throwing himself off a ledge. It was heavily guarded by celestial beings for privacy, and thus dangerous for the uninitiated. The others in that expedition also had "accidents" and bouts of madness. Archimedes survived and helped a man in Iquitos to start a clinic utilizing 78 herbs, some grown in the Amazon and others from around the world, that cured cancer and AIDS. I visited the clinic and tasted the drink of immune-boosting herbs they provided and enjoyed the baths.

I dreamed also of Tibet and an underground city near the Potala, as well as the Ural Mountains of Russia. Mt. Shasta in California also has two underground cities. The Amazon had various doorways, and the sacred cave of the Xavante Indians was a very important entrance for Matto Grosso, Brazil and the future.

Stories are told about the many entrances in the Amazon to Inner Earth. The Xavante name means "Guardians." Tserete had told me that his tribe was the guardian of an entrance way to an inner civilization that was very advanced spiritually. His cave entrance was now blocked. It was not time to enter physically.

The Valley of the Blue Moon has a doorway near Puno in Peru. That second group followed a ley line that protruded from the earth like a huge anaconda snake for half a mile, leading to a series of rock formations that told an ancient creation story. At the end of the walk was a perfectly carved-out door in the rock side of a steep hill. The door was huge, built for a giant, and had a place to give offerings to Pachamama or Virachoca.

It seemed like an old form of transport. Standing in front of the stone, we could enter the Valley of the Seven Rays. I could feel my etheric body enter the door into the Amara-mu-ru. I wanted to learn how to bring my whole body to that place and see the consequences.

CHAPTER 7

Bolivia

Kahlil Gibran wrote, "Your pain is the breaking of the shell that encloses your understanding."[1] I knew that Chiron had led me on this Violet Bardo to face what I disliked most in myself and others. Chiron calls us all to give up our inflations and sacrifice our false sense of immortality. After Peru, I decided to visit a small town in Bolivia known for its local shamans and sorcerers. Charazani, Bolivia was a turning point for me. It was there I learned about sacrifice.

Many traditions have a history of animal sacrifice, and in Bolivia and Peru it is common in shamanic practices. The Christian Eucharist is an example of a symbolic human sacrifice. In the Catholic Church, parishioners "eat" the body and blood of Christ. Here, sacrifice brings us closer to Christ in a tangible way. Any sacrifice is a communication to the numinous worlds of spirit, through the mediation of a valued object, to bring about a healing or a greater awareness of the connectedness of all living things. We are rebalanced in some way when a part of us is sacrificed to benefit the whole. My own inflated image of shamanism was sacrificed in Bolivia. I sacrificed my naive ideas about looking outside of myself to shamans—or anybody else—for answers. I had to give up glorifying shamans and native healers and putting them on some kind of pedestal. I had to learn to be more humble. In this case my inflated attitude needed to be sacrificed for the sake of wholeness and the restitution of my tour group.

In 1995, I led a tour to Peru and Bolivia. Our expectations of meeting powerful shamans in Bolivia were thwarted, perhaps by our need to overdo spiritual experiences. This is a brief account of our stay in a quaint small town full of sorcerers.

In Charazani, Bolivia there lives a simple man who bakes potatoes with his wife and family, and performs shamanic rituals with the coca plant. A guide led us to this village known for its medicine people. The town has a primitive hot springs and lodging, and creates beautiful handmade blankets and textiles. I brought a group of people there on a pilgrimage to see the practices of the local people.

As we were guided to the shaman's house at night, crossing a small stream in the dark, we had high expectations of an authentic ceremony. The shaman's home was lit by candles. It was sparse, but clean and neat, awaiting our special arrival.

First, he checked the coca leaves, divining any issues our group may have had and a course of action. The leaves only pointed out one difficulty. He passed around coca leaves to chew. He admonished us to chew half-a-dozen at a time. He then passed around a few cigarettes to smoke. Most of us did not smoke or approve of it, but we were polite and took drags, hoping it would add to the ceremony. Next he passed around 99 proof alcohol in a seashell. Most of us were nondrinkers—many had passed through AA—but still, we were in a ceremony and acted accordingly. It was like grain alcohol, and people began to choke and cough.

In the awkward silence, he passed around thick red wine. We took swigs from the jug, again being courteous foreigners to these rites and wanting the spirits to approve of our behavior. This was shamanic etiquette. The former members of Al Anon and AA drank round after round of wine. Soon, the air was full of cigarette smoke and the smell of liquor.

The shaman then produced the fetus of a dead llama, which is sold in the markets for specific medicine people and curanderos to buy. The fetus looked dry, small, and withered. He put cotton balls on leaves with little brightly colored candies. He poured holy water on the cotton-ball candies and read more coca leaves. He compiled one cotton-ball fluff for each person present, allotting us one candy each. The air was thick, heavy with death and spirits. More cigarettes, more shots of liquor were passed around. People began to grow impatient. After hours of coca-leaf reading and then cotton-ball constructions and talks with the spirits, the shaman was the only one gripped by the proceedings.

He asked for questions. One man asked if the cotton balls were intended for each of us, and if so, could they heal whatever negativity he saw in the coca leaves. The shaman remarked that we would walk outside together at a specific hour and burn the cotton-ball altars. But we had to wait for the right hour, and that was hours away. Another member of the group asked how long he had been a shaman. We all expected to hear that he had been one for many years, but the interpreter said, "one year."

Everyone began to squirm and cough and wonder what was really happening. Was this right? Was the interpreter mistaken? How could he have been a shaman for only one year? A few people began to refuse the fourth round of 99 proof alcohol; a few dared to reject the cigarettes. Most of the group had chewed at least 300 coca leaves.

Finally, after hours of repetitious prayers in the candle-lit glow—with the group sitting uncomfortably on the bare floor wanting to feel more than a hangover or a nicotine fit—the shaman got up and left us for a brief moment.

He returned with a cute guinea pig. The group loved the animal and was distracted for a brief interlude. The animal was being held by the neck; everyone was wondering how they would cradle or take care of the shaman's pet guinea pig. We all felt something auspicious was about to take place.

The shaman firmly held the guinea pig by the neck and with one sharp thrust of his knife split open its neck, pouring blood on the floor and the cotton-ball candies. He declared that the signs and omens for the future were excellent. He ripped out the neck and the guts of our beloved mascot and showed us how fortunate a group we were. He ripped out its still beating heart, and we all went into post-alcoholic shock!

Everyone rushed outside to throw up as wave after wave of nausea gripped the group. Most stomachs were upset from the animal sacrifice, but others of us were doubled over from the cheap wine, the cigarette smoke, the stench of dead bodies, and the taste of coca leaves, coupled with the 99 proof alcohol.

Still our guide and interpreter persisted, telling us how honored we should feel to have been invited into this shaman's house and to have had a guinea pig and a llama sacrificed for us on the same day. This was very auspicious. Everyone swallowed their distaste. We were polite but very sick. A few days earlier, we had ventured to the Inti-Rami festival of the Incas in Cuzco, enjoying the brightly colored costumes, the dances, and the multitude of Inca descendants. We had watched this high Inca ceremony from the walls of Sachsayuaman. Then, to our shock and dismay, came the sacrifice of a live llama. The Inca priests tore out its heart, blood spilling everywhere. We all gasped, but this was an ancient ceremony and who were we to judge? Sacrifice of the guinea pig was quite different. We had all known guinea pigs as children, and this brought up the death or loss of pets, or even family members, in childhood. It was personal.

Finally, the shaman, sensing our restlessness and horror at the slaughter of the guinea pig, ushered us outside for the big event. He chanted ancient healing prayers in a foreign pre-Inca language, while we each held our candles and particular cotton-ball altars. Unfortunately most of the group began to lose their balance at this point, probably from the 99 proof alcohol, and began lighting their cotton-ball altars before the appointed time. Their hands instantly caught on fire; they dropped the cotton fluff—the altars—and then they scrambled nonsensically on the ground for the remains. This was performed with awkward grace so as not to be disrespectful to those present, especially the shaman and our guide.

Finally, when all the altars and remnants of the cotton-ball-candies—some now badly burned—were gathered, we burned our karma individually and collectively while gasps of delight rang out—delight that the ceremony was now close to ending. We were wrong.

(Our patience had already endured a sleepless night when the temperature had gone below freezing, with our sleeping bags and tents suited for summer weather; also there was no true breakfast or dinner being provided. We had become slightly irritated with our guide for this inconvenience, but we assumed that Charazani and this shaman would more than make up for the discomfort of our journey. We had also decided to be spiritual pilgrims, releasing our need for vanity and creature comforts.)

The shaman next told us to bury the sacred llama fetus, wrapped now in herbs, on the roadside at a specific place to insure protection for our group. Cordial to the end, we gulped our last 99 proof alcohol, smoked another pack of cigarettes, and thanked our shamanic friend with heartfelt gratitude.

Needless to say, our walk back to town was tipsy at best. Many stumbled and fell into the stream. We thanked God that it was all over and that we were protected. Everyone faced how truly spoiled we were and how ridiculous life can be. The alcohol numbed any response to the ceremony, and therefore served its function. From the coca leaves, we were both sleepy and drugged, and awake in the darkness.

At the hotel, with our sleeping bags firmly planted on top of the sheets to ward off lice, we fell off to sleep while the Incas and our guide performed another fire ceremony, singing loudly into the night. The air was full of spirits. I slept, knowing that I was protected and that nature was strong, raw, wild, and full of sorcery. The whole town seemed to be casting spells, talking to spirits, and releasing curses and entities.

Our group awoke early in the morning, gathered our possessions, fired the tour leader, and left on a long arduous bus ride to Copacabana, Bolivia, to stay at the best hotel there. We had decided to pull out of our tour and visit the Islands of Sun and Moon instead, cutting short our visit by three days.

I did not have a total hangover, and on my morning walk I greeted townspeople with a smile. I felt that the crazy ceremony the previous night had somehow opened us to a strange world and that this ritual was our visa. The town had a strange light, full of magic. It was time for me to leave the sorcery to others. I wanted to be human, simple, without spiritual ambitions, and accept my life and its everyday beauty after the ordeal of Charazani and the smoke-filled shaman's den.

CHAPTER 8

Travels through the Violet Bardo

SÃO PAULO

A famous medium in Brazil had a huge, annual meta-physical conference in São Paulo. She would pay for my plane ticket and accommodations if I went. I embarked on a 747 for my first excursion to Brazil. No one spoke English on the flight, and everyone thought I was Brazilian with my dark, curly hair, and brown eyes. The stewardesses were amazed when I could not speak a word of Portuguese.

Studying the faces of my fellow passengers, my heart and sensuality began to open. Everyone was incredibly beautiful and sensual, and seemed carefree, but they also had a personal and collective "victim" consciousness.

Over the next days, I witnessed the wide division between rich and poor in Brazil, and their diminishing middle class. The poorest people live in shantytowns of corrugated iron and scrap wood, called favellas. The very rich have multiple estates and own most of the land. I was told of one wealthy landowner that owned 90 percent of one Brazilian state, monopolizing all the commerce and controlling most of the people who lived "under" him. He kept the poor of his land very poor.

I was told by Brazilians that in the northern part of the country there is much lawlessness and corruption.

Seven thousand people per week stream into São Paulo from the north to escape a low standard of living, and extreme poverty bordering on starvation for many. They hope to find success in the city, but many leave defeated after only a few months.

São Paulo is twice the size of New York City, expanding at an alarming rate, without urban planning. It has the largest population in the world after Mexico City, which it should surpass by the year 2000. The nicest areas are the Jardims—translated as the gardens—and Morumbi with its sophisticated shopping malls and parks. Downtown commerce is focused in Jardim Paulista; people born and raised in São Paulo are nick-named Paulistas.

Brazilians are fun-loving, joyful people. The poor do not show their suffering as in other parts of the world. They smile in a full, nonchalant way. There is a sense of martyrdom in everyone, including the rich who never feel they have enough money and remain insecure. I attract-ed many trusted friends, lovers, and companions on the path to spiritual freedom in Brazil. I have never loved a people as much, or felt as at home in a country.

Despite São Paulo's immense size and its traffic, I loved the people with their immense capacity for love, sensuality, physicality, and joy. It was very intoxicating. At my hotel, I played piano for the guests at night. I was astonished by their warmth and interest. In the morning the people working in the hotel would greet me and tell me some story of their lives or some spiritual insight they had received. We all felt a camaraderie and closeness for each other's souls and a need to share our respect.

After my opening address to the conference, I sat on a panel of presenters with huge photos of world Masters above me: Kuthumi, Saint Germaine, Master Morya, and Christ. Finally someone told me that my speech had been completely misinterpreted by the translator. She had not gotten one word right!

That night, I took my friend to a Brazilian jazz club. She was distressed that I, as a spiritual person, would go to a nightclub. She judged me as being imperfect. No one there knew how much I loved music, any music. The nightclub thrilled me with its eleven jazz musicians, incredible virtuoso vocals, and drums playing samba, bossa nova, and African rhythms. I was in ecstasy from the sheer skill of the talent assembled, but my friend only commented on the chain-smoking audience, the amount of liquor being consumed, and the low consciousness. Finally, she said that Saint Germaine told her that we must leave.

The veils are very thin in Brazil, and spiritual self-delusion is rampant. Yet, miracles happen there like nowhere else in the world. Spontaneous healings, strange manifestations of light, and extreme forms of clairvoyance are commonplace. My friend was constantly telling me how Saint Germaine guides her every move—where to stay, when to make a left or right turn, how to run her business. It felt more like possession than clear clairaudience.

On the day of my big speech, I requested a good translator. I also met a person I knew from Santa Fe. He was a well-known healer, medium, and clairvoyant in Brazil named Ricardo. His speech was before mine, and after a man from the Santo Daime community near Mapia, on the Amazon. They each gave clear basic instruction in shamanism. The Santo Daime speaker explained the workings of ayahuasca. When my turn came, I sat on elk and tiger skins surrounded with the bones from the medicine bags of the Santo Daime shaman. I faced a huge audience of a few thousand people. My heart burst with anxiety, and I felt the supersensible world give me the words to speak. All of my soul and heart filled the auditorium. I wondered if the audience could feel the angels in the room.

When I finished, the audience leaped out of their chairs and gave me a thundering standing ovation. They stormed the stage to shake my hand. I shook a thousand hands from the stage that day and felt the presence of Sophia and Archangel Michael in my aura. My friend tried to usher me off the stage, while the swarming mass of bodies pressed against me. I felt a profound serenity, the deepest kindness. I just wanted to give and give light and let miracles come. The whole conference was altered for me. Only nine people came to the first workshop, but I gave those people my best; the next workshop had sixty persons, all from word-of-mouth of those simple, courageous nine souls.

Later, Ricardo drove me to Embu, a quaint section of São Paulo. Here craftspeople, artists, and writers lived and worked. Ricardo had two friends there who made light sculptures of stone and crystal. One of them was a poet and the other a master of ikebana, the art of Japanese flower arranging. I loved them both from the first moment for their sensitivity in feeling and discourse—the souls of artists living in this present world and finding each other. Every painting, every stone wall in their home spoke to me in the language of sensitivity and art. The food, though simple, was full of inspiration, creativity, and love. Embu tasted good. It was the gateway to a new delicious world for me.

ALMADA IN UBATUBA

On my second visit to São Paulo the following year, I met a treasured friend and colleague on the path, named Carminha. She had started a center for shamanism and the study of Candomblas, the Nigerian religion of Yoruba and the Orixas. Umbanda ceremonies are Brazilian but with African roots, involving music, trance, and spirit-possession. The *orixas* are the greater beings of nature, such as Oxum, guardian of waterfalls, streams, and rivers—who was my primary orixa. My secondary helper was Oxossi, fierce warrior and guardian of forests. Other orixas include Yemanja, guardian of the ocean, and Nana, the grandmother, and Exu, the guardian of the gate, who cuts off the astral lower body for clear clairvoyance and protection.

Carminha and her friendly husband became surrogate parents for me in Brazil. They honored my work, and I respected them with deep affection. She was a strong Leo lioness and often had to step out of her own way, but she kept her balance. She helped many men and women to be empowered, artistic, and fierce. She had studied with Michael Harner and had visited Esalen numerous times. Carminha helps people to enter nonordinary reality for problem solving, healing, and therapy.

Her approach is very Jungian. She takes her students through various initiations with shamanic journeys to discover their personal spiritual teachers and for practical well-being.

Almada is where the profound initiatory work is done. It is down the coastline from São Paulo near the ravishing, picturesque port of Pariti. Almada is a nature preserve with a few fishing families in a tight village. Carminha built a refuge of small buildings into the side of a cliff. One room has the cliff built into its side with the towering rock face fully exposed. My room was a simple round tower of brick and stone. It was my little castle in Brazil. Views of ocean abounded as did African trees, large stone cliff expanses, and bamboo groves. It was a magical location for facing the shadows of the sacred and learning the technology of ecstasy for real self-discovery.

One evening in Almada, lightning hit the ground while I was leading a group in holotropic breathing and rebirthing. The ground shook, and the lightning gave everyone an electrical shock. The lights went off, and in the darkness we died to our old selves and lit candles of freedom. Lightning initiated this whole workshop, along with the driving rain and thunder, to purify and radically awaken us as a group.

We threw sticks into a large bonfire to burn our karmic misdeeds. We hiked blindfolded through the cliff-side jungle. We bathed in the water of Oxum, singing to the sacred waterfall filled with offerings of flowers to the Goddess. Here I was initiated by the orixa of lightning called Eunsun. The women of Eunsun took me into a large bamboo grove and hit my body very lightly with bamboo sticks, shouting chants and bringing me into the secrets of lightning and true warriorship. The women of lightning guided me to accept the courage and strength of Eunsun.

At Paz Geia the trees began to converse with me through the spirit of the forest and its guardian, Oxossi—a warrior of the trees and vines. He is the rising smell of dark decay, the trees that visit us in our dreams. Oxossi instructed me many times to take branches full of leaves and wipe them over my students' bodies to purify them. He explained that the severed branch is his symbol, because once cut it can regenerate and grow again into new life, a symbol of his hope for humanity. He told me how every tree is known by its fruit. A rotten tree, like a rotten person, bears rotten fruit. He says that a twig must bend to allow a tree to grow larger.

I learned from him how life is duality: creation and destruction, gain and loss, becoming yourself and being diminished back into the earth. He explained how trees link generations, outlast human beings, and are the time-keepers of Earth's history. He was full of wisdom, and I sat in his grove on Carminha's land and felt his presence reassuring me that humanity and the forest have a sympathetic identity.

He was very "real," alive, virile, and vibrant. He was the forest of Brazil. I felt like a white bird resting in a great tree. The waterfalls of Oxum brought me power, abundance, wealth, purification with a gentle touch. Oxossi gave me the stability and rootedness of the organic unfolding, maturing, and disintegrating of plant life. Death was always near him. He held the seeds of death and new life, and taught that death was in the realm of the dormant seed and not an apocalypse of hopelessness.

I would dance at night in Oxossi's grove of trees. I would strip off my clothes with the coming of the rain and feel the co-existence of stone, plant, soil, vine, bird, and insect under one canopy. Oxossi's world was my secret garden—a place to dance in the moisture of the forest. My two personal orixas or protector gods were Oxum, the goddess of water, dissolution, and movement; and Oxossi, the warrior of the trees that line the bank of a great river, the soul's final destination. Oxum could take me to the waters of life, but Oxossi helped me climb the tree into the unknown arms of the Creator.

Oxossi showed that each of my fingers was a different tree. I remembered in Celtic folklore that the thumb is the birch, the forefinger the rowan, the middle is the ash, the ring finger the alder, and the pinky, the willow. Oxossi said that trees give the hands their energies to heal. The fingers are channels of energy and the fingerpoints release energy. We can choose to hurt or heal, or to move our hands in sacred positions as oracles. I watched my hands change position, with energy bursting through my fingertips radiating in all directions. Oxossi taught me how to focus my energy through my hands by thinking of a particular tree. I remembered that the name Chiron means "hand." The art of chiropractic healing is the art of healing with the hands. Chiron is the teacher of complementary medicine and surgery and the use of the hands to channel divine energy. Oxossi became one of my chironic teachers that day.

I had previously learned a little of Sangoma, the African tradition of special herbal use, curing rituals, divination, visions, and dream interpretation, but I had never been exposed to Umbanda. Strange spirit possessions happened in my workshops for the first few days in Almada. Participants writhed on the floor, foamed at the mouth, talked as mischievous children or as Native Americans. I had seen the Yoruba priestesses, dressed in white, dancing and falling into trances, but it had never occurred in my workshops. Each of us had to become more conscious of outside influences and not fall so easily into possession and trance. I had to work hard to ground my students with their feet rooted firmly on Earth, and to open their heads to the stars. I wanted them to speak with animals, plants, and spiritual beings but still be in balance. Each student was taught to integrate everyday life and business practices with spiritual work.

In Almada, I performed a wedding ceremony for two friends from Campo Grande, in Matto Grosso do Sul, a state to the north. The wedding was a celebration of the inner marriage of Christ and Sophia and of their committed relationship. Relationship Yoga is a demanding, rewarding path using the transformative power of loving relationships to develop personal individuality, to know one's strengths and weaknesses, and to effectively deal with challenges in the world. Two years later—to the day—I performed a different wedding ceremony in São Paulo under a simple tree ringed in rose petals. It was a ceremony honoring the demands of marriage and relationship, responsibility and conflict resolution.

At the latter ceremony, the whole audience consisted of conservative, reserved Brazilians. None of them knew what to expect of a shamanic wedding ceremony. To our delight, many felt it was more real than a traditional church service—honest without affectation. They were moved in a solemn, personal way. The married couples held each other after the ceremony, honoring the vicissitudes of their union. They felt the day was an affirmation of family, values, morality, and marriage, and they had also learned tolerance of new forms of spirituality.

In the United States and Europe, it is difficult to bring people into their hearts without skepticism, and into clairvoyant attunement and visionary upliftment with discernment. In Brazil, people fall into trance states in seconds and enter supersensible worlds and deep states of consciousness almost immediately. Brazilians, however, were still learning a conscious understanding of these gifts, and also how to test the spirits talking through them. They had to become mature adults spiritually and not act like children. They were ready.

Spiritism of the nineteenth century is alive and well in Brazil. Psychic surgery is as commonplace there as it is in the Philippines. Brazil has numerous spiritist hospitals and clinics for healing. I once visited a spiritist center in Rio de Janeiro called "Lar de Frei Luiz." It is quite large and the work includes de-possession by earthbound spirits, the use of higher spirits for etheric healing, higher spirit diagnosis of disease and ailments, and the ways to handle materializations of spirits. There are schools devoted to the work of Allan Cardec, the nineteenth-century spiritualist who wrote volumes on his encounters with the other side. His books are now more popular in Brazil than in his home country of France. Possession and talking to spirits are so common in Brazil that many people go to Umbanda ceremonies on Friday and Saturday nights and to the Catholic church on Sunday. A statue of Saint Barbara protects the home; a certain plant wards off the envy of the evil eye; a woman is brought in to exorcise a house from Macumba curses or black magic.

AIURUOCA

Arco-Iris introduced me to Minas Gerais, a state of farms, cattle, and luscious rolling green hills. We worked together in Aiuruoca, a small town known in esoteric circles as a power point for transformation in Brazil. Aiuruoca and neighboring Mattatu are centers that draw people for meditation, purification, and ceremony. Dawn Eagle Woman and I teach there every year.

In one gathering, I worked in a bamboo grove next to a small waterfall. Eighty people hiked in—each as a segment of a white snake—to a large, powerful waterfall in total silence, with the sound of the falls heard in the distance. Each segment of the snake had a leader, and there was a follower at the end of the line. Everyone took personal responsibility for the people in their segment. The town of Mattatu had expressed concern about the hike, feeling that a line of eighty people would both be disorderly and ruin the natural surroundings. They were proven wrong. We took care of the earth and blessed the ground we walked on with each step.

When night came, we had to hike back—eighty

people in line holding a rope in near total darkness. Many were on the verge of panic. First someone twisted an ankle and had to be carried. Then silent fears forced some participants to hold the rope too tightly. The test was to trust everyone in the line—as if it were a single being with many parts. The rope was our link in the darkness to cross bridges and streams and find our way in the wilderness. It was a testament to group courage that we succeeded. The night gave us new eyes to see: We saw through our feet and kinaesthetically walked home.

Dawn Eagle Woman and I faced many attacks from unconscious participants in our workshops in Aiuruoca. Many tested our authority and, against our orders, took psychotropic mushrooms, which we later banned completely from all our work. One woman on mushrooms became psychotic, stripping off her clothes, and telling us the story of how she and I were married in another life and would marry again in this one. Stark naked, she told a two-hour story of a past life in which the whole group was involved.

In her discourse, I was a French explorer and she was the head of a native tribe. I married her and lived with the Indians, learning medicine ways. Her tribe came under attack and was slaughtered. A few survived and she wanted revenge. She never got her total revenge on the white people and was now taking it out on her own psyche through her mental illness.

In a talking circle, no one can be interrupted if they hold the talking stick. She held the stick too long, so now we have time limits. Later, she tried again to monopolize the group and was told fiercely to step down and pass the stick. She agreed. Many learned to finally speak up that day and learned to be leaders. A group must work together for the benefit of all, to not let one person dominate. She became obsessed by me, asking participants to come our wedding. She took off her clothes to speak but also to seduce. By telling her story of another life, she wanted to magically possess me and make a bridge to this life. I had to say, No!

Power gravitates to sex, money, and religion; here I experienced how people are attracted to spiritual teachers and the need to project their desires on them. I learned to not be so naive. First, attraction is not love. It is fascination and comes from our patterns of learned behavior in childhood. Second, the glamour attraction of the teacher is not a true bonding but glamour by association. Third, many women and men were attracted to me in Brazil, but I was unavailable. Why are we attracted to unavailable people? When attraction is not reciprocated, obsession and possession of the love object begin. I had awakened passion in Brazil, and I needed to learn how to take the emphasis off me and place it on the true work and teaching.

Despite the difficulties in Aiuruoca, I loved the land, nature, and the bountiful butterflies; but I was also aware of the mistreated horses, the inner politics and land corruption, as well as the cocky roosters who were used for animal sacrifice and fights. They always strutted a little too defiantly.

The land of the Xingu and Xavante tribes breathed with their vibrancy. I remembered living there in another time period and living in harmony with the natural world. Many sites were familiar. That harmony grows and stays inside my heart and has borne fruit. Aiuruoca and Mattatu was my homecoming.

CURITIBA

In Curitiba, I stayed by a lake that gently overlaps into another lake, graced by herons, ducks, frogs, dragonflies, and white regal ibis. My friend and translator, Pookie, was honest, friendly, and created a calming environment to live and conduct work.

Curitiba is where I blossomed. A Japanese-Brazilian flute player serenaded us at night with lilting finesse. The cows slept to the rhythm. The water flowed. We anointed our bodies with paraiba oil at night and put it in our tea. (It is the sap of a rain forest tree and builds immunity.) We sat in a hut dedicated to an Indian chief and meditated. A hummingbird built a nest in the ceiling and gave birth to its young.

I worked in groups of forty people a day, working two days and taking the third to rest and then repeating the same cycle again. During one workshop, one of my promoters brought her family, and I gave them extra attention. I showed them how to prepare for the immediate future with strength, how to overcome adversity, and how to see the gift. My promoter died shortly afterward, but her family had been prepared in that workshop. I remember her smile, her wit, her love of José Argüelles and his wife, her compassion and her worry that her family would be all right. She had brought them to the workshop to unconsciously prepare them for her death.

Many come to me to prepare them for death. I see the impermanence of life. Sometimes, I have no detachment; often I cry in my hotel room, after a long day's work, for those I will never see again. I miss my promoter who loved Curitiba and lived there, caring for her family before her death.

In Brazil, I began to enter into a bardo state or transition similar to death. The "bardo" can denote any transition in life or death from one consciousness or level of awareness to another. I had asked in Brazil to end all my karma from the past. I was seeing through my own illusions, sexual obsessions, and numbness. I had upped the ante, raised the stakes, and my inner work began to spill out into my outer life.

I remembered distant times in past lives and times in this life when I took the wrong course and went out of control. I became aware of falling asleep in my body and could feel a velvety numbness like a thick, swirling fog descending. Brazil reactivated an ancient time of past helplessness, hopelessness, and disillusionment. Soon I began to explore my previous lack of tenderness toward myself and others. I felt a deepening comalike numbness, and my breathing became erratic or nil. I had to make an effort to breathe into the dead space inside and breathe out the past denial and lack of memory. I did not know what I was denying until I began to breathe normally, retrieving something mute from a prebirth state.

The violet bardo is the transformation caused by the shedding of the skins of memory, and by emerging from a cocoon of swirling numbness into true feeling. This sequence of related events took years of active relaxation to unravel. I had to enter the roller coaster of the bardo and breathe through ancient pain to a breakthrough. I had to hold on to fears and then go into a coma state just to face them. Vigilantly, almost blindly, I knew to choose love over fear. Brazil prepared me for the great reckoning of my soullike death in life or as I call it: the "violet bardo" of purification.

BELO HORIZONTE

The third largest city in Brazil, Belo Horizonte, is located in the heart of Minas Gerais. My promoter was a young man who spoke with an ancient Native American Master. He had learned to conduct Native American rituals and had recently become a pipe carrier of the Lakota-Sioux. All his associates were youthful, vibrant, and sincere. They owned a metaphysical bookstore. My promoter, their ring leader, had a picturesque farm in the country. I loved his farm, the power, the simplicity, the horses, and the medicine wheel. A solemnity and quietness pervaded the house, and I talked to trees, to the guava, avocado, and corn.

His guide had brought me to them, and I honor their spirit of learning. An old Native American lives in their souls and reminds me of New Mexico and how far I am from the land I cherish. Brazilians feel a kinship with Native Americans. They honor their spirit and wisdom.

The rich of Belo Horizonte live on the highest hills overlooking the city in houses with elevators. Ostentatious, empty, and imposing, the houses of the rich are right next to the largest slum (favella). The main park of Belo Horizonte is massive, but dangerous if one is walk-

ing alone during the day or night. The overlook is peo-
pled with drinking and carousing individuals. I was sad-
dened by the decadence of the city. Outside my window,
male prostitutes were having sex one night. I yelled
through my window for them to keep quiet and to move
somewhere else. I prayed for the people to find the nobility of the soul beyond wealth and extremes.

I turned off the television, the music, the noise, and
found another current, a balance in the cacophony and
urgency of the city. I saw how the media seduces the
viewer with seduction, obsession, and power. I felt its
numbing effect in those prostitutes. I saw in Bangkok,
Thailand, how the prostitutes play power games with
their clients and seduce them for money and power in
the sexual act or in strange performances in night clubs.
I felt how numbed we are by pornography, and how to
watch pornography is to enter the power dynamics of
the participants. I saw violent thoughts, fantasies with
no limits being acted out. I vowed to breathe through my
numbness and yearn for love. Underlying all my need for
power was a direct yearning for God and for God's
incessant, true yearning for me. I opened my heart in
Belo Horizonte, breathed through the deepest coma of
numbness, reexperiencing all the accidents over the
span of my life. I saw many instances where I was overwhelmed by situations and felt helpless, hopeless, and
disillusioned, resulting in shallow breathing that strangled my life.

As I mentioned earlier, I had dreamed of dying by
drowning in a previous life while holding a statue of the
Black Madonna in a boat during a town festival. No one

had retrieved my body from under the ocean in that life, and therefore part of my soul was still trapped underwater, unable to breathe. I had been hung, guillotined, strangled in past lives and now realized that the throat is the primary location where we take in life and leave the body at death. An explosion went off in me, and I saw that a pattern was repeating itself. I had to stop controlling my breath and open my throat—not be afraid to take in life.

Months went by before my jaw could relax. I had to stop drowning in numbness and isolation. I had to feel my body and get out of my mind. My mind had an innate fear of water, yet the majority of my planets are in water signs in my astrological chart. I had to dive in again. I woke up in Belo Horizonte and breathed until my body tingled with awareness: I breathed out the anxiety reaction of panic and breathed in God's love and acceptance to change. I found hope again and learned to stay with the process and not give up.

BRASILIA

The site of the capital of Brazil was an empty savannah in the early 1960s before an entire futuristic city was built there. The city reminds me of the television show, *The Jetsons*. It is an architect's dream. Every road is planned. All the government buildings are in one area, the shopping centers in another, and the living quarters are separated for convenience. This city also has the highest suicide rate in Brazil.

My Brazilian promoter took me to the *Templo da Boa Vontade*, translated as the Temple of Good Will. It is the center of a metaphysical religion founded by Alziro Zarir. They receive huge donations, and the temple is lavish by Brazilian standards.

The main entrance is a huge marble pyramid with a magnificent crystal in the center point of the roof. A gigantic spiral, in black and white granite, is etched into the floor. In silence, we took off our shoes and walked the spiral to the center, where a solid gold square is placed. We faced *God's Throne and Altar*, an abstract sculpture by Roberto Moriconi. When entering the spiral, one walks on the dark granite in a counter-clockwise direction symbolizing the difficult journey to the center for balance. Returning on the lighter spiral is to discover the light in a clockwise direction. This is the path of moral and spiritual values reached by human beings, ending at the "throne of God."

The rest of the building is filled with gardens, memorials, silence rooms, art galleries, fountains with crystals, and water flowing through aqueducts. The Egyptian room is my favorite. My friend and I have dubbed it the "blue room." We paid an admission to enter like an amusement park. But it was well worth the donation.

Magnificent violet-blue rugs, altars, and paintings etched in gold fill the room with authentic Egyptian temple ambience. The velvet, blue-violet chairs are richly appointed and relax at specific angles for astral travel. Here, groups of people were sitting in remote sections of the room, astral-traveling and renewing their spirits.

I sat on a beautiful Egyptian couch, with the lights dimmed and specific Egyptian-inspired music playing in the background. A huge throne stood before me in gold, roped off to the public. The ceiling was painted with constellations of the Pleiades and Orion, along with Nibiru and other planetary spheres. I slipped into another dimension. Egyptian deities, including Anubis, introduced themselves and took me to the Guardians of the Threshold, who questioned all my motives and actions. They showed me my ego, my shortcomings. They sliced off my lower astral body with a sharp knife, and took me to an altar to drink wine and eat bread—a kind of communion of the Paraclete.

Egyptian figures escorted me through a dying ritual. I recapitulated my entire life, viewing key ritual events on a screen. I quickly proceeded to the Greater Guardian of the Threshold. I bowed on the altar and saw Sophia as Isis, revealing herself to me and taking my place in the ritual. She walked through double doors and led me to a cosmic Christ, as radiant as the Sun and joined in a marriage with Isis/Sophia. I perceived the cup of their union, one I can taste and breathe. Archangel Michael came and led me through a lion-faced room where I had to fight the lion and subdue him. I then faced a dragon and, with Michael's assistance, I saw my own dragon and emotional nature. Last, I passed through the fourth dimension of animals and saw plants and elementals. I then witnessed a journey to the stars. The Pleiadians showed me different star alignments and the origins of electricity, and I saw the path of Nibiru and its effect on humans. I passed through a triangle formed by Sirius, the constellation Ursa Major (The Great Bear), and the Pleiades. They gave me radioactive minerals to touch, and I was facing a strange looking being called Ahriman. He was unhappy with my progress beyond the material form. He tried to burden my levity with stones and gravity. I became transparent ether. I was slipping between dimensions too quickly. I wanted the will to slow down and to remember, to ruminate on the journey of Self.

Next, I faced Lucifer who wanted me to be a sexual, sensual, ecstatic Dionysian and enter various mystic trances and be a medium. I rejected his offer, and he was disappointed. I saw self-deception, illusory worlds made by Lucifer. I chose not to live in a fantasy world. I then was escorted through an abyss, a Void. I could have entered crystal cities and seen marvelous sights, but I rejected them. I chose to stay here and have one thought of belonging to everything. I then did a service of weaving and discovery, an imaginary work in other worlds. Imagination is the key to the etheric.

My friend sat up and tapped me on the shoulder. "It's time, Foster, come back. Earth calling Foster." I immediately come back, refreshed and changed. My friend whispered, "We have to leave for Alto Paraiso now."

ALTO PARAISO

A three-hour drive away was "high altitude paradise" (Alto Paraiso in Portuguese). As I approached, the sign on the highway read, this town is "The heart of light for a new civilization towards the new millennium." My hotel room was called the "diamond room" and was filled with Tibetan *thangka* paintings and watercolors of angels. The bathroom had an image of twins ascending to a Great Light.

That night I gave a talk in a large dome enclosure

ringed by water. We walked on a river stone path over still water to enter the dome. It was lit from the floor, which cast a somber, ambient light. The dome was a huge onion-shape in white, and I loved its simplicity and design. Here I sang a song to the Logos, a song I had heard in the "blue room." I seemed to be moving from temple to temple. I felt the quality of commitment in this room as we told stories of *Jumping Mouse* and *The Handless Maiden*.

The air was clear in Alto Paraiso. Many people were actually walking around talking to different spirits and gods, channeling the cosmos. At least that was what my guide and my promoter told me. "It's a crazy place full of channels, visionaries, and power spots. Here, many people talk to extraterrestrials, especially the children." I seemed to fit in perfectly. I made fun of my access to other dimensions. It is a serious pursuit here as well.

We spent the next day at Solarian. Mila, our guide, fixed us a nurturing lunch of food from the forest floor. She preserves the land as a caretaker, planting rose bushes, vegetables, and trees, talking with the elementals. She guided us to the "Archangel Waterfall." First we had to cross a bridge—with 45 people in tow—made of twigs and bark. The elevated bridge was situated over a river with rapids. Only one person at a time could cross the bridge as it shook and made rickety noises. It was unstable, multileveled, and slightly dangerous. It was an initiation, and I practically jumped across with excitement.

The waterfall was so huge that we could not go near it. It was pounding with noise and energy. We all stood there in awe, amazed at its Archangelic Presence. The waterfall lured us into the water to swim and to sing prayers to the might and grandeur of creation. We adorned our hair with leaves and carried staffs made of branches. We hiked back delighting in Paradise.

During my workshop, two people entered with no intention to pay. They disregarded the pleadings of my promoters and stormed into the seminar, moving all the paying participants out of the way. The next day I called a council to confront them.

Calling council is an ancient tradition of confronting another person by building an altar to the possibility of the relationship. The altar stood between the two parties, and we were instructed only to talk to the altar when it was our turn. Two people on either side mediate the conflict. The person who called the council speaks first.

I explained the situation fairly and remarked how this council was unique in that I would open the floor for many to talk. The couple who had walked into the workshop without paying, whom I will call Saul and Luna, wanted very much to be part of the group. He said that he did not have any money and that he would give me a gift of a necklace instead. He meant no disrespect. His girlfriend cried, saying that they both were misunderstood. Next, my promoter spoke of not feeling respected. It was his test to finally take a stand for self-expression, authority, and rules.

Next came an avalanche of women. Evidently, numerous women in the group had been Saul's lovers. He was accused of dealing drugs, of taking women's energy, of stealing power, of being a paramour, and of dishonesty and seduction. My friend, Samvara, who lives in Alto Paraiso, felt personally attacked by Saul when he addressed their disintegrating friendship. She had assisted and supported him, and he had betrayed her many times. Samvara is a woman of honor and beauty. She fights with detachment, honesty, and passion. She is a great guide and teacher for many Brazilians. She loved Alto Paraiso, and she challenged Saul with her force of will and her compassion.

Each woman, some yelling and weeping, told of their past seduction by men, and how these men had taken both their life force and bank accounts. Seduction, they learned, was not love. That was allowing themselves to be manipulated and be used at vulnerable moments in their lives. They went through the process to say, "No more." They found the courage to mature and make clear boundaries as to self-respect and self-worth. They learned how self-esteem, intuition, and discipline in love are important attributes in a woman's life. They would not be fooled again, falling in love with the idea of love, or falling in love with a man's potential, not his actual everyday self. They would not be naive women.

Saul was shaken to his core. He knew his seduction patterns. He kept saying he would change, but his actions spoke differently. I told the whole group my personal issues with seduction. I explained Saul's distrust of authority, especially the brutality of his father. His need for strong men in his life was sabotaged by his acts of self-pity. I told him to have a peer group of men who were sincere, strong, balanced men to repattern the paramour habits of his father. He had to stop being his father—having affairs while married—and abusing his son. Saul, the son, took after his father and abused himself. I explained how I had sabotaged myself through seduction and had learned to admit my failings, patterns, and to act in a clean way. We spoke about how men must say No to affairs, to stealing associates' girlfriends; of how seduction is mother-bonding, needing to get energy and sustenance from women. It drains women of their love like a vampire. How insecure and fearful men can become when "losing mother." Saul spent his energy tricking everyone else to get attention and more attention. It was never enough. He felt unworthy to love himself and he needed mirrors of adoration around him. He even believed women's projections on him.

Saul and Luna were not allowed to stay in the group, by a close vote. The whole group participated in a democratic way. I offered him forgiveness without judgment, and spoke of patterns and family systems. They were grateful. It was up to them to embody the experience, to get the lesson. Other people left the group that day. They confided in me, "I came for that moment when I could step into my rage at him and let it pass. When the truth about him came out, I understood my role as seducer. I felt totally vindicated and healed of my own patterns in the council. Now I can move forward in my life." I hoped to do the same.

Then, I wanted to separate my private life from my work. I needed companionship and stability in my private life. I created clear, distinct boundaries and upheld them. My work in Brazil flowered and grew, and I left that continent with a full, disciplined heart. I finally loved myself, and I was allowed to be loved by many people.

I let the love grace me inside. I had close friendships with men, a peer group to review all our actions and thoughts. We stayed firmly on the path of self-questioning and illumination. With my male Brazilian friends, I could play and grieve. A Brazilian spiritual family had been seeded.

That country immersed me in the violet bardo. I had to transmute lifetimes of power struggles in relationships. The bardo is a time of dying to the old self without feeling numb, to conquer death through receiving God's love. Numbness is the predecessor of power, seduction, and obsessive behavior. Admitting the numbness is the first step. Breathing through it without forcefulness is the second step. Finding the time bomb inside and letting it go off prepares a person for the violet bardo, an avalanche of change. Brazil was my time bomb. I had gone there to end a past life of seduction, and for magical exploration. I had to clean up my sexuality and power issues to give that country my best work. I had to let the fathers die and not be ashamed to be their rightful heir. I had to let the old kings of power be transformed through the violet bardo into kings of love. The Holy Grail serves the Grail King. I had to surrender in an active manner to receive love as a gift, a miracle, claiming my healing to replenish my soul. This was the death of numbness, and the beginning of the deeper bodily breath of God in experience.

PART THREE

PURIFICATION AND SELF-DECEPTION

CHAPTER 9

The Dream of a Bull

The beginning was void. The first thing to be
formed in the heart of the void was a tree.
The first tree sprang out of a womb of energy,
and, emerging from its millions of buds, there
sprouted the whole of creation.[1]

-Maori creation myth

On my return to the United States, I began to see how
South America, and Brazil in particular, held the key to a
new kind of shamanism. Through personal and collective
upheavals, many people were thrown into traditional
shamanic initiations. There are ten of these initiations:
1) The breakdown of one's normal life and withdrawal
from the everyday world, followed by a retreat into the
spiritual caused by an illness or a calling to be isolated
and set apart from society for a specific time; 2) a battle
with one's own demons, or as the Greeks call them, daimons. Here, the psychological, spiritual, and physical trials begin with a review of the spiritual aspects of one's
own birth or prebirth experiences; 3) possession by
archetypal realities or spirits who initiate one into a vol-
untary experience of dying. If the shamans do not honor
these spirits, they later face them in other people, often
through groups in conflict; 4) a realization of one's own
woundedness from childhood. Early feelings of abandon-

ment or lack of love from a guardian or parent arise—the psyche is vulnerable at an early age, before the ego is fully formed, and open to the imaginal realm; 5) descent into the unconscious for a prolonged period followed by a return from the Underworld with a dream of birds or animal allies helping the spirit to return to the body; 6) the birth of social concern for others and their souls' evolution by opening one's wound and releasing its potential to heal others; 7) an interest in or a pilgrimage to sacred sites to have visions of ancestors, spirits, and gods; 8) a discarding of outmoded ways of living. Compassion for one's self and others, and a new relatedness to all life, takes hold. A period of spiritual warriorship begins with special dreams or flights to cure others or to work with gifts of the spiritual world in healing; 9) a return to the community or the world one left behind to begin one's work and training with humility and grounding in nature. The healing of repressed instincts continues as the shaman finds the threshold between opposites and lives there. Shamanic or chironic healers must continually face the chaos of their own mental processes and learn a new form of communication between mind and instinct; 10) acting in accordance with the rainbow, a harmony of heaven and Earth, bringing new meaning and awareness into the world, with discernment. Here, one needs boundaries with others and time for rest, renewal, solitude, and celebration.

After Brazil, my own personal trials had just begun. I, too, had to face the repetition of my early childhood emotional patterns in my relationship with my parents. Chiron is the teacher of these new shamans, healers, and practitioners of a new kind of complementary medicine. He began to prepare me for the trials ahead.

Chiron first showed me a sycamore tree in a dream. He told me never to pass a sycamore tree without recognizing its spirit. I was instructed to tear off a sycamore fig from a branch and to watch a bright white milk flow out.

He told me how trees assured women's fertility and watched over their children, keeping both safe from destructive spirits. Chiron explained how in the past women sought fertility from willow and poplar trees, spreading gifts and offerings of prayers under their boughs. The tree itself was a woman who needed to be anointed with oils, fragrances, adorned with clothes, and decorated with abundant flowers, and who must be honored at the birth of a child.

The forest was a place of vast, deep silence where elders went to die or be buried under huge hollowed roots. Many trees were carved as burial tombs to carry the dead over the waters on their way to rebirth.

As long as a tree's roots are deep, so is the length of its life. Trees became sacred dwelling places of ancient gods and spirits, holy places of awe and reverence. The earliest forms of temples were trees. Trees were once the center of village life. Sitting in the shade of a holy tree granted inspiration and wisdom. At one time, trees were more sacred than human beings and to harm one could cost a man his life.

My love of the violet forest was explained to me by Chiron. He told how the tree is the Eternal Mother. She is a safe refuge, a shelter, feeding her children. The conifers—cedar, pine, cypress, spruce, and redwood trees—make the world green and exist today as they did hundreds of millions of years ago. They are constant, changeless, ever green, and a symbol of the enduring energy of Earth. He spoke of the Tree of Life, the Tree that remembers all ages and makes them one.

I understood that in the future I would live in a home in New Mexico by the banks of a river, surrounded by large elder trees, and would plant an orchard for long life. This would root my experiences in Brazil and reveal to me how the inner pattern and design of the world regenerates itself.

I asked him why I had to go to the jungle, and he explained that some healers are fire shamans, others are rainmakers or wolf, eagle, or bear shamans, but my gift came from the forest. This was the time of purification, to connect to God through my spirit and to the wisdom spirits of the trees.

Chiron taught that chaos precedes creation, cosmos, and birth. If I wanted to see in a new way through the violet forest, I had to see how I resist chaos in my own life. He said, "Chaos is the substance of the *prima materia*, the alchemical work of transformation. You are like two fishes bound together swimming in opposite directions beneath a tree in a majestic forest. You will deceive yourself and pull your heart into two pieces. You will discover your own emotional manipulations and, at the same time, your transcendence of opposites in a confusing confluence of forces. One fish wants to remain an individual, and other fish wants to destroy that individuality and remain in the wine dark sea of the womb. How can you not be taken away by the material and emotional chaos that ebbs and flows throughout your life? Do not ignore these tides. I am the forest, where the tree's deepest powers are lifted highest to keep you from falling into the sea. Just when you establish an inner order in your life, you become preoccupied with it and are submerged once again into chaos.

"Never feel that you are truly special. What you need is the power of the bull, the primal phallic strength. Sacrifice the bull of needing to be special and important. You need a separate individuality and power to enter your life. To eat the bull, you will be faced with your own selfishness and its powerful will and destructiveness. I, Chiron, will connect you to pure instinct, and you will have to find your own male voice and authority. You will feel envy for people who have a solid identity. You will try to absorb other people's individuality into yourself.

"Confront the people you attract who desire comfort and compassion, but who make unceasing demands on your time and energy. Have strong boundaries and be imbued with the power of love. You will learn to voluntarily surrender to that power, and the forest will enter your soul.

"You will need time for creative sanctuary when your sensitivity leaves you feeling drained and overwhelmed. First, you will face unseen enemies, deception, and disillusionment. Nothing is as it appears. Let that be your motto. In the end you will sacrifice your need to suffer to be whole.

"Eat the bull. This will give you the strength of the warrior."

The first months after my return from Brazil were

filled with dreams of wild bulls. The first involved an image of a bull being sacrificed at my feet. At first I did not want to touch the blood-stained animal. I felt it was barbaric, and after subsequent dreams, I began to feel ill. I was avoiding my destiny. I finally ate the bull but did not own its power inside me.

I know that in Crete bulls were ritually sacrificed for the people to partake of instinctual fertility. Bulls were highly valued in ancient Greece, and a prized bull was often asked of a king, for a sacrifice to a god or to take in its essence with the proper prayers. In my dream, I had to eat the bull and incorporate his masculine strength through a prayer to its spirit in all people.

For weeks, floods of emotional moods, stubbornness, and deviousness absorbed my thoughts. I then led a series of workshops where I faced the bull I had eaten. My first challenge after South America came in the person of Gitte White Hawk.

CHAPTER 10

Gitte White Hawk

Chiron told me, "Your deepest wound is with the Great Mother. Witness her in destruction and see what she is not. As a child, your wound was giving your mother the power to be the wounded woman, the wounder and the healer of wounds. You gave her an unholy power over your life. You felt her moods would annihilate you, and you learned never to confront women, fearing their rejection. Learn a division between you and her for your own preservation. A child can mold itself after whatever a mother wants, losing its identity in her ocean. Separate your wounded mother from those you come in contact with. These are the purifications of the forest."

"You vil have a gud time, everyvun!" were the first words Gitte White Hawk uttered as our group of thirty-three people arrived at Puye Cliff Dwellings campground. "You vil all act like Indians!" she said in her heavy German accent.

We had all come to San Felipe Pueblo to have a feast with Gitte White Hawk's spiritual mother, a kind Native American woman. She was busily preparing the food for the next day—corn, peppers, and venison. Gitte and I had met through friends. She had left Europe years earlier to be trained in Native American ways. Her mother had been a tyrant, disinheriting her and making her life miserable in Lichtenstein. She had moved to New

Mexico, and for many years she went on vision quests and did sweat lodges. After meeting her spiritual father, she had settled into living a simple life among the Native Americans.

The tyrant her mother mirrored to Gitte was still alive in her daughter. Gitte always had little money but she made beautiful Indian medicine objects. I decided to give her a three-day job of instructing my group in Native ways. Since most of the group were foreigners like herself, I thought she could be a bridge. I was dead wrong.

The group arrived late, and Gitte was furious. How dare we keep her waiting! I apologized, but it was difficult coordinating thirty-three people for three days in the wilderness. Gitte's assistant was very mad with me for infuriating her teacher. This was not going to be forgiven easily.

The first of seven hidden lessons this group learned from Gitte's behavior were: 1) Never be on "Indian time," and 2) you will be judged for being late. Next, Gitte sized up the group like a military leader and then built a fire for all of us to share. The people in my group, from six different diverse countries, told of their love of nature, their sincere quest to learn Native American ways and to be of assistance to Gitte in the next three days. She was pleased with their sincerity. We all retired after dinner to our tent city to sleep. The evening had been congenial.

Medicine Month is a three-week training that Dawn Eagle Woman, her husband Brian White, and I created. Each day a new training occurs, most of which are subtle clearings of the different bodies—emotional, physical, mental, and etheric. When Dawn and I work together, we have no agenda but what is best for the group. Activities include mask-making and the dance of the masks, journeying with the drum and journeying into past incarnations, visualizations, sweat lodges, a vision quest, mindfulness practice, shamanic body postures, sacred dances, the art of seeking visions, warrior training, and the making of the body painting—where a person lies down on the ground and another draws the outline of the body with pastels. Next, the person looks down at the body outline and relates the personal stories of the wounds and painful patterns, then sketches them on the outline. The whole group hears the stories and myths of each individual's life.

Other processes involve releasing anger and rage in a healing way, learning the use of flower and plant essences and aromas, leadership training, and healing in imaginal realms. The men leave for three days to hike in the wilderness and discover personal freedom, and the women have three days of incredible self-healing while differentiating the deep masculine and feminine. The whole event depends on the willingness of the participants to trust the group and to put aside personality differences so as to bring peace to conflicts, understanding to ignorance, and love to fear. We see how experiences can illuminate the way to spiritual realization but can also embroil us in self-deception. The group becomes a vast mirror of the Self, as each imperfection and slice of unconsciousness is heightened and exposed.

Gitte woke up the next morning and surveyed the activities of the camp. First, she told people not to meditate or to practice yoga as this was Native American land, "her" land, and the spirits would be unsettled. Next, no non-Indian music could be played on "her" land. Also, little flesh should be seen during the Corn Dances. Men should wear long pants and the women should cover their arms and knees and not be disrespectful to the Indians.

I have lived in New Mexico for years and have visited countless pueblos, but had never heard anyone make these claims. Our next inner lesson was that, 3) Native Americans "own" land. They *are* stewards or caretakers of the land but no land is private, or exclusive, as Gitte was suggesting. Certainly, this was not her land but the Pueblo's and the Park Service's. Lesson 4) was that Native Americans are intolerant of meditation, stillness, mindfulness. Gitte objected to the East Indian influences when the group was learning Native ways. Lesson 5) was that Native Americans cover up their bodies. At the dance, most of the audience wore shorts and T-shirts because of the sweltering heat. I saw a confrontation brewing.

We had a lovely feast that day, pottery demonstrations, and a huge Corn Dance. I had paid fifteen dollars a person for the feast as a donation to the tribe. Gitte wanted more. She did a blanket dance, where she threw a blanket on the ground and hopped around a bit, expecting us to throw money offerings on it. This dance was repeated several times until Gitte had enough finances. She quickly gathered the blanket up and walked to her tent, while we stood stunned. In lesson 6) Gitte gave the impression that Native Americans are greedy. It was Gitte who was greedy, not the Indians, and she had just crossed the line into abuse of authority.

We were all about to burst. Gitte then decided to divide us into two groups—a simple Machiavellian technique of divide and conquer. She took the more advanced students (in her eyes) and walked them into the hills for a pipe ceremony. She told this small group that I did not know what I was doing, and that she felt Dawn was kind but ineffectual. Of course, only Gitte knew what was right and appropriate. Through the pipe she bonded to this small group and opened her power to dazzle her new apprentices. A hawk flew over their heads, confirming Gitte's "discernment" and control of the situation.

One member of that group was a prominent shaman woman from Salvador, Bahia in Brazil. Upon returning from the pipe ceremony, she came to Dawn and me and told us, "Gitte is a shaman teacher of hate. She is teaching me how not to act. She is abusing her authority and laying the seed of her own destruction through intolerance. We are here to confront her with compassion and show a true way of love. We are here to be shamans of love." Dawn was silent, awaiting her moment to reverse the situation and trusting me to find a resolution.

That night two Heyokah warrior women in the group decided to paint their bodies in black and red and put sticks and leaves in their hair and body suits. They looked like wild nature spirits, wild women of the west. They screamed through camp and danced furiously around the fire to exorcise their rage at Gitte.

Gitte said the dance was irreverent to the spirits of the land and had divided the camp. She never took responsibility for her own division of the camp, always playing the inflated medicine woman. Her assistant was again fuming at me for allowing the dance to occur. Lesson 7) was that no one in a tribe is allowed to be themselves or to offer a differing opinion. We all had to listen to the "chief." Any dissension would "anger the spirits."

The next day the whole camp was disillusioned. Gitte was their ruthless tyrant. First, she tried to teach us a native dance in her flaming black and red spandex outfit. The dance was very simple, and Gitte made it so complex that almost everyone gave up. She then blasted us with a diatribe on tape by a Native American man in prison denouncing white people for taking his culture. His hate was tangible. Gitte was crying, agreeing with him, and demanding that all the white people return the lands "we" had stolen. Gitte forgot that she was white too. The hypocrisy was so thick that you could cut it with a knife. The whole group stood amazed, mouths agape.

Finally the group decided to leave en masse if I did not confront Gitte. The rage and anger of the group entered my body as a conduit. We made a final huge circle, and I explained to Gitte that she had acted as a ruthless tyrant.

Next, participants in the group started to explain to Gitte their perception of her denial, repeating her various side comments, and telling how it had split the group. Then, the group turned on me, blaming me for exposing them to this charade, and I exploded! From the depths of my soul, I explained how we were all responsible for this lesson, but that I would at that point confront Gitte on her abuses of shamanic power.

I told Gitte that it was my responsibility to fire her. I needed to confront her as my surrogate mother. I had to value myself and the group and take action as a man, no longer in my mother's shadow. I had to stand on my own feet and protect the group.

I forgave her and explained that we were packing our tents and leaving at this very moment. Gitte was visibly shaken. She had thought I was weak and would never stand up to her authority and her need to control. She took it all personally. I told her that we thanked her for teaching us what not to do as medicine people.

Finally the group was satisfied and united by my outburst of anger. We all embraced Gitte and gave her parting gifts. We forgave her individually and as a group. Gitte still felt that she had done nothing wrong. We all walked away, and I vowed to be a shaman of compassion and patience. My own training had been with ruthless tyrants who had threatened me, and Gitte had brought the whole group into that experience, challenging us to own our power and take decisive action. I released a tyrannical energy in my own body and psyche that day and found a profound nonviolent peace, but Gitte was only the first test.

I faced my fear of confronting my own mother when she was impatient or passive-aggressive. I had never felt it was appropriate to stand up to my own mother. In many respects, I let her moods dominate me. I let her have power over me because I did not have adequate boundaries with her as a child. Gitte had played a mysterious role of shocking me out of my old habits. She was a gift.

CHAPTER 11

Hawaii

Chiron next told me, "Become like the oak tree, the king of the forest. Mistletoe, a parasite, can grow on the bark of the oak, and is an unearthly plant between heaven and Earth. When the Druids cut the mistletoe from their sacred oaks at a specific time of the Moon, they wrap it in white cloth and sacrifice two white bulls. The pairing of the two is a mysterious manifestation of the life force. Each person who accompanies you on a journey is a pairing of energies. Learn from those drawn to your work. See what must be cut and what must be sacrificed. Find the mistletoe and oak in any relationship."

With the onset of the new year, I had planned to facilitate a small workshop in Hawaii for ten people to purify ourselves. I chose the garden island of Kauai because there the ancient Hawaiians were deeply connected to nature. Upon arrival, I visited *heiaus* or outdoor temples. I could feel the island's innate sense of balance, order, and reverence at these natural temples. Stones were wrapped in ti leaves, as prayer offerings made to the gods, and placed on platforms made of skillfully placed stones upon which the temple structure was built. The warmth and the aloha greeting of the island wrapped me in gentleness as I watched dolphins and whales from the balcony of my hotel room.

I could hear in the ancient chants of the Hawaiians

the nobility of *ali'l*, or Hawaiian chiefs or noblemen. I saw how women and men now shared power and responsibility in a balanced way. The *Kumukipo* is the great chant that records their ancient version of creation. From the original darkness to the gods descending to Earth and creating light, all is recorded in this chant with exact genealogies. These are the people of the rainbow who understand the three worlds of the mystic: the higher, the middle, and the lower selves, and their lineage from the divine. I felt that there I could learn more about the wounded healer and how to help others with their childhood wounds.

Kauai is the oldest of the main islands and is represented by a lei, a necklace made of flowers, shells, or ferns. Kauai's essence is represented by the mokihina lei which is violet in color. The Mo'o Kahuna, the priests of Ku and Lono, are in charge of ritual and prayer. These powerful priests keep the secrets of the old traditions. The healers of the island are called the Kahuna Lapa'au. They can cure many diseases through a deep knowledge of herbs, an understanding of how to reverse lava flows, and an initiation by ingesting a poison without dying. They know how to contact the life force and the *manas*, or energies, of the spiritual world, and seed them in the physical body. Here, in this garden paradise, I felt the group could relax and find peace. I was completely mistaken. Nothing in group workshops turns out as is expected.

After two days on Kauai, I became very sick. I stayed in bed dreaming only of my own repressed instincts. My life force was under attack, and I sensed that this trip would be the death of my old self. I dreamt of the Na Pali coast, perched 4000 feet from the sea, and the rain on Mount Waialeale. My consciousness was filled with a strong undertow of water as if I were submerged under the coral of the island. A hurricane had blown through the island a year earlier, and I could still feel its powerful forces unsettling my dreams. A strange upheaval in my unconscious began, as I had convulsions, sweatings, and fevers. Paradise was not what I had expected. I dreamt of destruction and saw the Hawaiians dying of diseases brought over by white people.

When Captain Cook first arrived in Hawaii in 1778, an estimated 300,000 people were living in harmony with nature. Within a hundred years, only 50,000 remained. Their lack of immunity to the newcomers' diseases, and their dispossession from their own land by the foreigners, made many Hawaiians bitter and dejected. Today, the aloha greeting reclaims the real spirit of the original Hawaiians' simplicity, beauty, love of nature, and acceptance of foreigners. Yet, I felt my whole being in revolt, wanting to leave before I had even gotten settled.

The spirit of the forest came to me in my dreams, reassuring me that this voyage was necessary, but I felt as if I were on a boat in a rough sea, rocking back and forth with no control. I could feel the power of the land dreaming through my body—the heliconia, the royal Ilima trees, the pineapple, avocado, and mango fruit trees. My body began to reject the fruit, the change in diet, and this immersion into a different culture. I was feeling torn apart. I knew that something momentous was about to happen.

The group arrived a few days later. I had planned to have a friend cofacilitate the workshop, but with such a small group, I felt it was unnecessary. In the end, I really needed the help. One woman had brought her grown daughter to Kauai, and I first worked with the girl's woundedness with the mother. She was unable to commit to a deeper relationship with a man; an aspect of her relationship with her mother needed to be healed first. Many of our emotional wounds come from our early relationship with our mother because, although we need her to survive, we fear her terrible power to deprive us. We want to devour her totally so that she will never leave us. To heal this wound, our group craved good mothering, and in Kauai we all were searching for the motherland, the abundance of her feast and nurturing bounty.

All of these insecure childhood feelings reemerge in our adult life when we crave power, sex, fame, money, food, status, and fusion with another person—to become someone else. If other people bring up a strong reaction of love or hate, we feel at their mercy, afraid of the devouring nature of our relationships. We want to incorporate into ourselves the object we desire. Here we need a separation from the mother, along with true forgiveness. We have become an all-consuming society in need of differentiation from the mother.

This workshop set the theme of my work for the next year—sexuality and habitual seduction, birth, death, loss, abandonment, and emotional destructiveness, followed by rebirth and regeneration. People in this group began to come into contact with where their emotional lives became fixated in infancy. Destructive envy, love, and guilty depressions surfaced in the workshop. To balance this shadow element, a deep well of strength, endurance, and vitality from the positive side helped us to feel safe in our group connectedness and protected enough to proceed.

I began to see my own patterns mirrored in the group healing. I learned how we control others to try to protect ourselves against loss and abandonment. We may hide our vulnerability behind moodiness or a facade of control—one man continually smoked, creating an visible screen between himself and the rest of the group.

Each participant in Kauai wanted to return to the deep womb of the Primordial Mother and to feel her darkness and cellular mothering. We examined what needed to die and be sacrificed in our old selves in order to be renewed. The rigorous control to protect others from our own potential destructiveness brought up feelings of unworthiness, of low self-esteem, and of being somehow defective. These destructive feelings can be projected onto others and incite paranoia, like having to ward off evil from psychic and sexual attacks, real or imagined. These threats may not always be personal in nature. Sometimes we assume the blame for the tragedies of others.

One woman accused a man in the group of making sexual advances toward her. She later withdrew this accusation, telling how she was dragged into relationships with men in the past. Her sexual abuse issues from childhood rose to the surface. She began to feel an incestuous seductive bond to me, and I pointed out her lack of boundaries with family members as a child.

As a group we explored love triangles, unconscious power struggles, and jealousies. Learning about power, its uses and abuses, was a common theme in Kauai. We had to peer into the darkness of our woundedness, an area that most people ignore. The sweetness and light of Kauai camouflaged the darker landscape of our past feelings of punishment and sickness welling up from the repressed unconscious. If we accept this darkness, then Chiron helps us to view it objectively, not to identify with or try to change it. We feel more at home in life when we confront the dark side in a conscious way. As healers, this group could reach people who felt trapped in pain and darkness; this was their gift. In fact, many who attended this workshop later opened up centers of healing in foreign countries.

The relationship between the mother and her daughter became a focal point of the group. Everyone adored the daughter, and the mother felt ignored. The daughter received her healing, but the mother could not. I took this woman on a hike to the Na Pali coast. Early on she sprained her ankle and could barely walk. I talked her into continuing; she cursed me but remembered how her parents had continually forced her do things against her will as a child. Her wound involved a lack of early love and bonding with her parents. She felt that she been her mother's victim, forced to be a certain way. The woman recalled feeling that she was never good enough in her own mother's opinion.

Another participant, her roommate, began to play the unconscious role of everyone's mother. I felt my own mother smothering me in her actions. Various participants became annoyed with her and accused her of controlling and judging. Her core wound involved acting as a scapegoat for all her mother's rejected feelings. Chiron, too, was rejected by his mother. This woman felt that her mother had not wanted her to be born. Becoming a focal point for everyone's childhood suffering, she began to have breathing problems and her health deteriorated. She was physically becoming the *group's* scapegoat, the human sacrifice for all our pain.

Yet another revealed that her mother had chosen her husband for her because she was secretly attracted to him. She felt deeply betrayed by her mother, and she later divorced this man. She then told of being sexually abused by her cousins. She needed to release being the love object for the people around her, to forgive her low image of herself. She had to release the years of power struggles with a husband who dominated her and whom she could not love.

An avalanche of grief and sadness pervaded our work on Kauai. One woman became uncontrollable, and in her rage toward her parents and her ex-husband, and her helplessness as a child, she began to tear clumps of dirt out of the ground in anger, sobbing for her loss of control.

Another participant assumed responsibility for the things in her reality she could not control, like being dependent. She depended on her husband to take care of her. She had brought him to Kauai in the hope that I could be a bridge to his healing and she could subsequently have more freedom. She carried her husband and children's burdens, hoping for a reward or recognition, but she was disappointed and refused to claim a new life for herself. She took on too much, failed, and felt guilty for not living up to her responsibilities. Her need for independence and power was suppressed through her shame and fear. Her husband was new to this work, and he felt uncomfortable with her expressions of loss. He denied that he had any problems. He gradually lowered his defenses when the thick air of the room lifted and some humor was interjected in our process. In fact, at one point we had a wild burst of uncontrollable laughter at the absurdity of it all.

During the workshop, each person in the group took on the mantle of the outsider or dissenter, as the person feared being taken over by the collective ideals, prejudices, and opinions of the group. Some were anxious to get their healing "right," trying to live up to some spiritual ideal. One woman felt she was trying to win over her cold, distant parents. She had become addicted to perfection, and so had to find an inner freedom and commitment to life, to allow the imperfect in her to live without attacking it.

Almost all the participants in Kauai were healers or had been involved in spiritual work for some time. Chiron displayed his tumultuous magic in our group. Usually healers bury their deepest pain and capacity for wounding by aiding others. The bottom half of us is a wounded animal, and the top half is the healer. Participants who identified with the wounded part of themselves became the outsiders, the victims, or the scapegoats who are traditionally banished or killed. When banished, they must fend for themselves. One woman, who had environmental illness, felt banished and victimized by the processing of the group and began to call home for some love and acceptance. She wanted either to escape or be left alone. I allowed her time to lick her wounds. The fact that she saw the process through was a huge blessing and a testament to her desire for health.

Chiron can work through an illness or crisis to bring up our bargaining wounds with God, when we sacrifice our health rather than give up a one-sided or inflated attitude. He can bring up, ad nauseam, patterns, complexes, events that we repeat in spite of our best efforts to change. This is how he teaches us to let go of what we are outgrowing. It feels like an unceasing struggle, when we just need to give it up.

Our first ritual of purgation involved writing down all our lies, fears, incompletions of the past—our feelings of loss, betrayal, persecution, and disillusionment. With all our secrets carefully recorded, we burned the papers near a Hindu temple. This temple, situated on the Waimea River, contained a huge crystal that focused intention. As sadhus worshipped all around us—under gorgeous banyan, banana, and kikui trees—we burned the past.

Our next ritual was to return to our birth and breathe through any trauma experienced at conception or at the moment of birth. The group experienced breach births, twins dying in the womb, fetuses aborted by their mothers, and babies not wanting to be born and hesitating to come out at birth. The experience lasted two hours and consisted of deep breathing, opening the womb, and crying for physical and psychological release.

Mothers in the group began to realize how much they

had become scapegoats for their own children. They saw their stifled creativity and abandoned careers sacrificed to bear their children and for the men they chose as husbands. Many felt they had done what was expected of them by their families but not what they had intended in their hearts. By admitting this loss here, they could then be friends with their children, and did not have to project their unfulfilled desires onto them.

Our next purification involved lomi-lomi massage in the ancient temple of Hawaiian healing. We had salt scrubs, steam showers, saunas, and dance therapy to move the pain out of our bodies. A team of female masseuses came over from the island of Oahu specifically to work on us. They felt our group was calling them to perform a ritual cleansing that would be experienced in the islands for a long time afterward. Every part of our bodies was massaged—including the women's breasts to release their inhibitions and fear of being touched. It was highly unusual, but the women began to love their bodies. The men were in ecstasy from being so pampered.

Our next purification involved dancing the hula. The hula is more than an ethnic dance; it is the spirit and soul of Native Hawaiians. Hula began solely as a men's practice in religious ceremony. It eventually was opened to women and was adopted by the theater and opera of the islands. The gentle swaying of the hips, and the subtle undulations of the hands and feet, tells a specific story. Also the chanting of the "mele" is an integral part of the whole synchronized unfolding of a tale. Every part of the body must be controlled, including the facial expressions. We had three different hula experiences, one incorporating traditional chants of the nobility. Each experience of the hula was more liberating and playful. With focus and concentration, everyone was beginning to heal through a connection with instinct, body, and land.

The climax of the workshop was a feast given in our honor by friends of mine who lived in Kauai and provided a Moroccan feast with mask dancing that culminated in a belly-dancing exorcism. First, we were all dressed in Middle Eastern outfits to play our respective roles in the dance. We selected masks to mirror our internal states. Our host was initiating us into the dance of our shadows, which represent what is repressed and denied by our conscious awareness. It is often in direct opposition to our usual mode of behavior or how we perceive ourselves. The group's shadow clearly reflected unresolved parental issues. Yet, the shadow actually contains our undeveloped potential. Since the shadow may be a threat to the ego or our perception of ourselves, the initial reaction is usually one of fear, anger, and rejection. Because the shadow is unknown, it is often projected onto others, which is often revealed by a strong emotional charge or uncontrollable response to a certain person or group situation.

The brilliance of our host in Kauai was his ability to enact archetypal dramas in the form of theater. In ancient Greece, a person would go to the Temple of Asclepius, a student of Chiron, and a founding father of medicine who could raise the dead and was punished for it. In Epidaurus, at the Temple of Asclepius, a person could see plays that spoke of internal repression and conflict. A visit to the temple at night would involve dreaming individual woundedness and finding a solution to its paradox.

Our ritual theater of purification was created by our host to cut the cord to our mothers and to find our buried instinct. He had us perform the dance of the mask and mirror. With a mirror in one hand and a shadow mask with animal depictions in the other, we danced out the group dynamics with each other. The mask was our animal nature, and the mirror was our perception of ourselves. We had to eventually reconcile the two, which led to a riot of belly dancing—a cathartic, wild, Gypsylike dance of abandonment and ecstasy.

Two belly dancers began a shamanic enactment of the unbridled emotions and woundedness in our group. They intended to unite our animal and "civilized" natures in a whirling mirror dance of self and shadow. Two Gypsylike women took on the suffering of our group in a series of very strong, gyrating movements. They were enacting a dance of our wounds and our opening to creativity. The women danced my issue of the fear of seduction and my dreams of the Gypsies. One participant's dance mirrored the victim and scapegoat issues for some of us, and yet other dances were for drug addiction, for sexual abuse, and for fear of losing a relationship and dependency on one's partner—all to help develop our own will. The last dance was the dance of the Chiron archetype, an exorcism of sacrifice to free us from our chains of self-involvement and excess.

The dancers practically collapsed after they had enacted our whole personal mythic drama on Kauai. I was grateful, relieved, and in awe of their work. The dancers themselves felt personally guided to do this performance and give this dinner for us. It was their catharsis too. We had now entered the domain of the wounded healer and would soon gain entrance into the hermit's cave.

Our host concluded the ceremony with his performance. He came out in the black robe of the night initiator, a hooded figure of magical import. He was a magician, teacher, hierophant, and hermit who arrived to cut us free from our old selves. He opened his cape at one point; the lining had mystical symbols and stars sewed onto it. He then flashed a knife to cut the astral and emotional debris from our etheric bodies. As his cape opened, he took off his mask and magically inducted us into another world. I felt queasy, as if I were witnessing an ancient initiation. Our host spun in circles for a long time and seemed never to stop. The room began to spiral upward, and the ground was opening beneath us. I began to fear the intensity of the escalating performance. Our host ended the evening with a loud shattering shout, and our stunned group silently left to recover in the privacy of their hotel rooms.

That night, at a heiau (outdoor temple) at the ocean's edge, we gathered around a large fire for the next ceremony, where we each burned a part of our old selves and committed ourselves to the path of the healer in the future. We played drums, sang, told stories by the fire, and invited friends on the island to participate.

Our host told us the story of his near-death experience with the elementals who came there last year to regenerate Kauai after the hurricane. During this experience, he developed his sense of smell to a very high degree. He spoke of how the royalty in Hawaii honored their navigators for their sense of smell. The navigators used the positions of the stars to steer their canoes and boats. They also had an acute sense of smell and had contact with devic beings, which helped them to chart their course. Our host explained how life is a journey on the sea of the unconscious—our soul, a little boat. To find grounding and instinct, we need our senses to open and navigate a path through the world. Where we begin our journey is where we will inevitably end, but hopefully with more compassion for the sacred night and day journey. The stars are our guiding lights by night, and the Sun our essence by day. Our spiral is to the depths of Earth's suffering, to be reborn in her womb, and to return with a new consciousness to the surface world.

He had brought us to this spot on the water's edge where he had seen the elementals of the four directions returning to Kauai after the hurricane that destroyed a great deal of the island. Many hotels were still boarded up, and much of the vegetation of this garden island had been wiped away by severe gusts of wind and rain. A great violence, like the exorcism dance, had swept through the land. People lost everything, including our host who had no hurricane insurance. The whole island was humbled by nature and experienced its own death and regeneration.

This humbling storm brought the people of the island together as a whole. People had to work together to rebuild Kauai. The old drug energy of dealing and consuming left the island with the hurricane. The complacency of the surfing rich began to change as they took a more active role in rebuilding their paradise. The writers, rock stars, Kahunas, hotel owners, had to put aside their egos and protect the fragility of the island in its rebuilding and rebirth. No more overdevelopment or emotional unconsciousness and devastating thoughtforms, which are what drew the hurricane there in the first place.

Practically every plant and tree had to be replanted. The people of Kauai had taken their Garden of Eden for granted and then had to wake up to discernment in thought and action. Preceding our arrival, Kauai had gone through this ferocious transformation. Through facing their Underworld journies and the storms of the past, our group members felt they had experienced their own personal hurricane.

Our host said that a new order of angels and devas had arrived on the island to begin a new process of planting and seeding. New energy was needed to create a heightened vibration of awareness on Kauai, one that would be a beacon for healers to trust their inner selves and to endure the trials of their own wayward natures. Kauai had to be exorcised by the storm, and amazing new lights were filling the plants. The Elohim and the Ophanim and the devas were regenerating the soil with a higher vibration and focus. Our host believed that he had to come to Kauai to receive new insight into his work as an alchemist.

Etheric energy was sweeping the island and reconfiguring the relationship between human beings and the land. I began to truly feel safe in my body, observing the hibiscus' deep red flowers, the kukui nuts, sweet pota-toes, guava, breadfruit, and coconut trees. I ingested arrowroot and chewed on the pepper plant. In my room, I began to spread fresh aloe on my skin, with *hinu honu*, a cure for windburned skin. I was attracted to tamarind and the taro plant. The whole island became a remedy for my ills.

We let in the etheric (spiritual) body of the island, the etheric substance of these new elementals, and they warmed our hearts and worked with us long afterward. We went to the farmer's market and ate the local pro-duce. We filled the condominiums with fresh food and flowers, inviting the nature spirits to cocreate with us. We saw how our own etheric bodies were changing and becoming stronger. Those who resisted became sick and confused, although they were still receiving a blessing. We invited the spirit of Aloha, of peace, inside our skins.

When it was time to leave, I thanked our host for his grace, support, and encouragement. He was a true friend. I left Hawaii thanking Chiron for our group expe-rience, and knowing that each participant would spend at least a year integrating this experience to encompass all the levels of profound change.

The eye of the hurricane is important. It is the calm, still place of initiation in the midst of the drama. I dreamt that night that two white bulls were sacrificed, and a magnolia tree invited me inside its flower and closed its leaves over my skin until I was ready to travel again.

CHAPTER 12

The Aftermath

In Hawaii I learned many valuable lessons. One was that personal grief and anger toward a mother who has not provided enough support can be often projected onto a scapegoat. My students, through sharing their childhood experiences, had revealed to me how a mother can fall in love with the divine potential in a child who becomes, in a sense, her redeemer. The child falls in love with the image of his or her spirit of divinity in the mother's eyes, feeling idealized in the exchange. As adults, these children look to parents, children, marriage partners, disciples, students, patients, audiences, for this same idealization, which becomes a very seductive experience. We feel tremendously healed of our flawed selves for a short time. Then comes the fall from grace. We feel a need for a constant "fix" of love and adoration from a new source. There is a desperate need to be idealized with our faults glossed over rather than being loved despite them.

The beloved, the person who idealizes us, reflects back to us a precious soul essence, the spirit of the divine which otherwise might never have emerged from the darkness. We want to be redeemed because we then can redeem our loved ones, and we become lovable as a result. We are filled with divine ecstasy because we feel we can redeem someone else. For a healer or therapist, this can become an addiction. Accepting our humanity ends the addiction.

What is true soul union and what is seductive enchantment? An idealized image of another leads us into darkness, promoting more pain and suffering. We can risk loneliness and accept our own mortality, like Chiron, when we begin to face what lies outside of Paradise. Hawaii brought up this image of a paradise that reflects our bonding issues from infancy. Most of my students never wished to be born. They wanted Paradise and enlightenment without incarnating fully.

I began to see how opening the doorway to the unconscious psyche aggravates childhood wounding for many. We have problems adjusting to the physicality of life and the body. We do not accept the darkness of everyday reality and would rather have environmental illness or chronic fatigue or an illness associated with being re-mothered again.

Love must be rooted in empathy for each other, grounded in our essential humanity. Too much empathy with no boundaries is unhealthy. We can moderate it by knowing our limits. A sensitivity to life's difficulties and inequalities is sometimes the result of experiencing our family's pain and disappointment as a child. Joy and pain are part of the inheritance of human beings. If the challenges in life are discussed, faced, met, then a deeply moving and guided life can begin. We often do not want to face life's limitations, being ordinary, because we would then lose Paradise and the false idealizations of others.

Many people come to my seminars with a desperation, a hunger to believe everything I say. They are attempting to find, through the spirituality of others, an acceptance, love, and perhaps a salvation, that they cannot find within themselves. I can only point the way to the One within who can fulfill their needs. No spouse, parent, lover, or audience can fulfill them. I have learned to distinguish between myself, the one I love, and the divine source. This is my form of redemption—to keep these distinct.

In the primal fusion of infancy, with all its erotic excitement, I could see the image of the loved one clearly. My mother was heavily sedated at my birth, though she denies it. I have had to break through these foggy, sleepy, dreamy memories to see clearly the one I love, and not desire that desperate primal union again, which drives many people to spiritual dependencies. Most people seek fusion through idealizing another. They want to return to Paradise, which is lost forever.

Real healing begins when we love ourselves enough to see the faults and wounds of our flawed humanity and to gain awareness through it. Couples are healed through mutual compassion for each other. The dying release this life through compassion for themselves and their loved ones. My goal is to see the workings of the whole psyche and give voice to its processes, so that individuals can reclaim or discover their souls and not surrender them to others. Personal responsibility in healing is paramount. *Self-responsibility was the key to healing Chiron's wound, the giving up of his immortality to heal himself.*

Chiron is similar to the Fisher King in the Grail myths, or to Christ. He heals, suffers, and dies as a human being so that we may all live. He is a comet blazing in the night to help humanity discover its gifts. He is not a saint, avatar, or guru, but a figure grounded in reality with permanence and constancy. He is the healer in all of us who helps guide mere mortals to a new level of consciousness. His link with Christ is through the trees.

Christ's whole life began and ended with the imagery of the tree. He took up carpentry as his vocation. The trees helped to shape his mind, body, and soul through his woodwork. He knew how to ask the tree for its wood to bless his hands. The tree taught him first to be focused and one with his art and material. He carved the spirits of trees. The trees then became symbols in the parables. He likened God to a great tree and himself as the vine. At death, it is the cross of the tree that he carries. This is the knowledge of opposites and how to balance them. He is crucified on a tree and dies like a seed returning to the Underworld. His resurrection is through the trunk of the tree to the branches of heaven. The Universal Tree aided him to accomplish each stage of his mission. The tree was his guide and protector to link the three worlds together.

The sap of the tree reminds me that a fire, life force that never burns, lives inside all life forms. That fire is kundalini. When activated it opens the psyche to the other worlds. I once dreamed that I was in a Maya temple, where many women had snakes in their mouths and were dancing to the rhythm of kundalini, opening the chakras to balance the energies in nature. Kundalini is a fusion within the self that encompasses the divine and nature, and still lets us retain who we essentially are.

Soul travel and shamanic initiation should never divert us from the path of our essential humanity, from facing our mortality and limitations. These enhance what it means to be a body—less a fusion with another, it is a coming home to the self.

One of the most profound moments in my life occurred a few months after my Hawaiian workshop, with my friend and colleague Dawn Eagle Woman. During a vision quest, in which participants do not eat for three days, remaining alone in the wilderness, an amazing sequence of events happened.

A vision quest often involves meeting your own inner teacher, after facing the trials of birth and submerged memories. You make your own circle in the wilderness, demarcated by branches, stones, or leaves. You cannot leave the self-containment of that circle for three days. Everything you need must be there.

To go beyond birth trauma, the vision quest symbol is the circle of life, the great hoop of creation, where you can be centered and wait for the Great Spirit. It is a second birth in which you create your own circle of life. It is a fusing of the small self in a small circle with the Greater Self, the Great Circle of the Cosmos. It is an active, responsible, vigilant experience of the awe and wonder in nature; you are then ready to participate in life with direction and vision.

Dawn and I had sat by a fire for three days, with one of us always alert and awake, during this particular vision quest. This wood fire is the eternal fire symbolized, the fire of kundalini, the indestructible soul that is our warmth. During the third and last day of our vision quest, a storm began to gather and we decided to call everyone back to our base camp, thus ending the quests.

Earlier Dawn and I had visited each person, taking each an ear of corn to eat. Corn symbolizes the soul and its resurrection from the Underworld. We asked all of them about their health and to report any visions. One woman said that she felt that a dark man from her past was stalking her. As a child, she had discovered that her mother was secretly receiving letters from an admirer and was having an extramarital affair. After reading her mother's letters, she decided to take action. She placed the letters where her father would find them. Her father eventually read these letters and became vengeful toward her mother. This little girl had betrayed her mother to punish her and to have her father's total attention, but her father filed for divorce, and the child was left with the guilt of her actions and a separation from her father. This had not been her intention. She wanted him to rebuke the mother and to be praised for her actions. Instead, she had to live with her mother in a state of denial. She later developed a complex that kept men at a distance, while secretly wanting them to possess her.

She became possessed by her inner man, who wanted to punish her for revealing her mother's secrets and to possess her with his violent anger because she refused to fuse with him. She adopted her naive childhood denial pattern, feeling that she had done nothing wrong. This dark man stalked her on her vision quest, wanting to get revenge for destroying his two marriages (her father's and later her husband's whom she left when he tried to possess her).

Dawn felt the gathering storm was connected to this woman's childhood feelings of guilt. The storm began to grow violent; hail and frozen rain pelted the ground. The woman remained frozen like a little girl, unable to understand her predicament. Her vision quest site was in an open field. Lightning could strike her because she was exposed entirely to the elements. Dawn and I ran to her. She was oblivious to the danger. The rain intensified. We waved our hands as we approached, hoping she would lie on the ground. Thunder cracked over our heads; the air began to sizzle.

When we arrived, Dawn and I instantly made a sandwich with our bodies around this woman. We put a rubber raincoat over our heads and hoped for the best. We intuitively knew that the lightning would strike there. I held the male pole and Dawn the female pole. We were in service to this woman who was naive to the forces in nature that she had stirred up with her repressed feelings.

This was a test of our faith in each other, that Dawn and I could be in complete alignment and protect those in our care. Did we really walk our talk? This was the true test of our working partnership. Would we sacrifice our lives to help a participant?

An equal matching of polarized energies was needed to divert the lightning. Then, in an instant, it hit! A jolt of electricity hit us, sending a shock through our bodies that our aligned energies dissipated into the earth. It took all our shamanic skills and concentration to perform this feat.

I felt the kundalini energy rise up in my spine, and I

accomplished my true mission in that moment—to be a bridge for others between heaven and Earth, sky and land; this happened through the medium of electricity. The three of us continued to chant and sing, as we lay in a frozen puddle of hail and rain. Thunder railed around us, but we harmonized our voices to respond to it. Exposed in the middle of a large sage field, we were the highest point for a half mile in all directions.

When the lightning hit us, we knew of our divine protection, our faith in the divine, and our strong wills. A terrible catastrophe was diverted, and Dawn and I were relieved.

Whenever Dawn and I are in alignment and perceive a danger, we ask permission to reverse the current. We protect the Earth and neutralize the dangerous forces of human neglect, denial, and unconsciousness. Our work is to bring harmony to places of devastation and confusion. The vision quest was a success, and we all survived the storm.

The issue of possessiveness is like a storm. Seduction is a foggy, murky zone of excitement and cloudiness. Since it is not love, it does not engage the clarity and consciousness of the psyche. It is a place of complexity and woundedness that must be stirred like a storm to be acknowledged.

In all subsequent workshops, I have reenacted that lightning experience and feel poised between land and sky, aware of my own body, to offer the most benefit to the participants. In the later seminars I had to learn more about my own naiveté and fear of possession by spirits.

CHAPTER 13

Possession

At the moment of our reconnecting with sexuality, instinct, and creativity in a deeper way, the underworld of possession invades the waking consciousness. Most people are unprepared for the bardo in life, this terrain of death, but it is the first stage of linking one level of reality with another. Disengaging from society for a period of illness can often be an initiation, and a sojourn into the chthonic depths, but too long an absence from one's vocation is detrimental. Possession may be the first threshold to cross on a journey of initiation. It is the first door to the dwelling places of spirits, demons, and gods.

I had been told that while on ayahuasca I had left my body vulnerable to attack by a dark shaman. I identified this shaman, but I could not rid myself of him. He was living inside my body, feeding on the astral matter. He was a parasite who did no work for the insights gained through his habitation. He thought he could learn from me through osmosis.

This was dangerous for me because he fed on my energy, making me tired and weak. This was active possession. I had an entity, who was actually a living person, inhabiting my body. He thought he could enter me, while I was out of my body on ayahuasca, and I would not be aware of his presence. He was wrong. A friend of mine, who releases attached spirits and lifts curses in his private therapeutic work, had identified the dark shaman during an evening at my home in Santa Fe.

One of my closest friends, who had studied anthroposophy and received Tibetan empowerments from a Rinpoche, wanted to help me. While I was in Brazil working, she would bring together four powerful people to create a strong enough field of protection, love, and conscious discernment to dislodge this entity.

At the prescribed hour, this group of four adepts met on the inner planes and identified the person attached to me. They asked Archangel Michael to assist them in binding the person's spirit and letting the angel release him from my physical and etheric bodies. That afternoon in Brazil, outside of São Paulo, I closed my eyes and met my friends on the inner planes. I could feel their intense love and protection surrounding me. They proceeded to detach the spirit. I saw through a fog, as if on a screen, how I had abandoned my physical body in Peru. I had been shocked by ayahuasca which detached my astral body. I then saw how this destructive shaman, out of envy for my work and wanting my energy and experience for himself, infiltrated my energy field.

At birth I was born open to the unconscious and had not learned sufficient boundaries. Due to an early lack of ego development and my mother's domination of me, I found myself susceptible to possession as an adult. As a child, I bonded to my father, despite his judgmental nature, by creating a corded relationship. I attached myself unconsciously to him to receive love in exchange for money. Cording and possession are part of weak ego development, leading to a dependency on others to fulfill one's needs. I would relinquish my will when fatigued or overwhelmed, giving up the inner power over my life to another. In my quest to reunify with my mother or to fuse with God, I confused spirits and other "energized" people with the divine. I was susceptible to possession because of my desire to merge with everyone without discretion. I had to learn to separate myself from the object of my love and from the divine. This is a separating out of psychic contents, which is essential to a healthy life.

I began sealing up all the areas in my aura where possession could enter through a weak definition of self, making a ring-pass-knot around me. We had to bind this dark shaman from Peru with the force of love and by invoking Archangel Michael for protection. He did not leave willingly. It took four powerful people concentrating on me to exorcise him from my body. I decided never again to leave my body on ayahuasca. I learned these lessons in a difficult way.

I had deceived myself in Peru through self-importance, and allowed a dangerous presence to enter me. While clearing this entity completely from my psychic field, I focused for two hours on the inner planes. I could feel colors penetrate me with healing. I felt the entity leave my body, and a profound peace was followed by a need for rest. I slept the whole next day, relieved to be rid of him.

I had been corrupted by the ayahuasca and what I later identified as the "Old Moon energy." I had to go through this to learn discernment, to gain a clearer understanding of the etheric worlds, and to learn to trust my inner teacher again. My friends' compassion and their spiritual techniques were guides to the supersensible realm of the shaman. Self-preservation and self-valuing were the next steps to becoming stronger and less of a target for invasion.

I was discovering my tragic flaws and seeing myself as I am. I was all too human and made mistakes, but I tried to correct them, in time, with a balanced spiritual approach. Living with real integrity, we never give in to being victims; we know that every action is a choice and has consequences. Energy, strength, is gained through the admission of our weaknesses, our mistaken actions, and our wayward thoughts.

The dark shaman taught me that stealing energy is a power control issue. Many people come to my workshops to steal techniques, or to fuse with my energy to gain knowledge for their own work. People will try to avoid payment for my services as a way to drain and deplete my energy and work. It is the law of balance in spiritual work to receive in equal measure for what is given. I ask for what my service is worth, and if people do not honor this requirement, I lose large amounts of personal energy and power from unbalanced exchanges. I try to help people put their energy where they can get the best results. Money is a way to direct energy. Where we put our money is where we get our results.

The dark shaman was hurting and destroying himself. Who can win in our power struggle with ourselves? The destroyer in our psyches who knows only power, because we never let in love as children or did not want to be born but to remain in the womb, fused to the mother? Or the redeemer in us who will atone for our past self-deception and admit our power issues over remaining unborn? I chose life and birth again, and affirmed my soul's right to exist and evolve in the physical world. The dark shaman taught me how not to use my energy, and how not to invade the delicate workings of other people's psyches.

Whenever we feel unclear, misty, and foggy, we are experiencing another emotional pattern rising to the surface of the psyche, and we cannot divert it by withholding our energy and attention. Also, energy will be called from the unconscious through the movements of planets and their magnetic fields of influence. We must integrate this energy or it will create physical illness, must clear the mist by acknowledging our secrets, discover the repressed contents of the unconscious, and take time to nurture our animal nature. Entering this domain will show us our wounds and how to help others with theirs. In this way, we face the dark intruder, demon lover, repressed childhood, family memories, and the denied circumstances of the past. Courage, faith, and steadfastness are important for success in this endeavor.

During a healing, many clients give up their power. They give up on living. They do not want to be healed. They go numb, catatonic, and cold. Their breath loses heat. They are lost in an event or state of miasm from the past. Their healing is locked, safeguarded, and blocked in the past. I cannot help them unless they take responsibility for their own healing process. They must fight the numbness and break through to the life-giving circulation of blood. Then I can jump in and finish the work.

However, many of my clients never get that far. They must have the courage to choose love and to trust someone, to feel worthy and to take responsibility for their yearning to be healed. Everyone is child of God, a miracle. Healing is an affirmation of the desire to be truly alive and willing to sustain life, breath, and body. It is an active journey to the Underworld to find the treasure of self-awareness and compassion for our human shortcomings.

I have witnessed many deaths, and each time I had to actively resist being drawn into the undertow of the dying, to actively reaffirm my existence. I grieve the dead too much to be sucked into the realm of the dead. To grieve completely is to release all numbness. I will not die because my father died. I will not die if my child dies. A small part of us may temporarily become numb until we face our loss and pain, and we realize that it is a preparation for the violet bardo. To peer into the darkness with physical awareness and sight is a form of resurrection and ascension, and a transition to a better life. In the bardo, this is the fall into matter to find the light of the soul that is hidden, unrecognized, and distorted by boredom, complacency, and the trauma of an unrealized self.

During my next workshop, in Colorado, the Violet Forest gave me another lesson about possession. My need to be special to my mother, to persist in the desire to unite with her, led to numerous problems in relationships and work. First, I would become like Dionysius, drumming, singing, telling stories, always followed by female devotees. In the Dionysian cults of ancient Greece, women would tear apart bulls in their frenzy.

Men can go through ritual castration and dismember-ment around these incited women. This is similar to the rock and roll era of the Sixties in which rock stars were practically torn apart by their frenzied audiences. These performers wore long hair like the Mother and were chil-dren of the Goddess.

I began to lose my boundaries with my work partner Dawn Eagle Woman, allowing her to mother me and pro-tect me from these women, a role she did not want to play. During this workshop in Colorado, a participant spoke openly about her distrust of groups and that she really came to "get my mind." She asked me to sleep with her and to have private talks away from Dawn and the group. She began to make the whole group uneasy with her demands for attention, and even tried to seduce Dawn as well by telling her that she was her greatest teacher.

The woman's moods began to shift into despair and exhibit narcissistic tendencies; she saw everything in the group only in terms of how it affected her. She refused to discuss her past because she felt that it was finished and she was "beyond it." Next, she began to openly challenge Dawn and curse her for mothering me and keeping me from her. She then spread rumors that I was sleeping with certain participants. Her imagination began to invent these wild scenarios because she was obsessed with having total fusion with me.

I felt the presence of the Neptune archetype in her need to have total devotion to and fusion with another person, to return to the state of womblike bliss. She took no responsibility for her actions and would not stop her insistence until she had achieved her goal. She began to call herself the dragon of the group, the chthonic feminine rising from the unconscious to fuse with her partner. I was certainly unwilling to have any such union, but she ignored my wishes. She could never see me clearly, obsessed with her own image of me. This was a way of avoiding her own needs, burying them in me and using me up before she moved to the next man.

She was angry at Dawn, a projection of her own mother's lack of love and bonding with her as a child. Her mother had refused her entrance back into the womb of love, fusion, and divine bliss. She now entered relationships with men to fuse with the divine. She needed to accept being ordinary and human, and to create art or work that would allow this acceptance. But she refused to believe in this remedy, and was convinced that she was a god, immortal, and capable of the greatest tantra.

The group grew impatient and voted against her involvement in certain activities. They wondered why I had not asked her to leave so that the real work could continue. I saw that issue as the scapegoat; this woman was the focal point of the real issues of the group. She manipulated the group because she could not get what she wanted from her mother and her unresolved issues were now projected onto us. We had to be her mother and accommodate her whims. She wanted total control but had no control over herself. She had eating disorders and lacked a deep, loving bond to her own mother, who was "eating her up." At one point the group had to search for her when she fell asleep in the forest. Her need to be continually rescued pointed to her earlier aban-donment as a child.

Finally, after getting nowhere and acting like a child for three weeks, this woman left the workshop, feeling dejected, wounded, and frustrated. She refused to say goodbye for fear of losing her connection to us. She refused real love and wanted a magical, idealized union at any cost.

I had attracted people to my own work through my charisma. Through association with that charisma, many people became inflated. I could now see the effect of my charisma on others and had to use it to lead people back to the divine in a more humane and structured way. I had to honor my own Saturnine limits when helping others to cross over to Uranian expansion. Chiron was teaching me to place boundaries in my work.

Many participants try to run away from group work-shops, mirroring their early childhood trauma in which one of their parents ran away from or abandoned them. This causes a split in the psyche, and instead of devel-oping an ego and personal identity, they now want to fuse with the other parental object or its substitute. When the obsession to possess me—or other group leaders—as the love object was refused, these people began to age, losing their youth and glamour, and their magical projections began to untangle. Personally, I had to be honest about my unconscious need to be liked and adored; I had to help people stop running away from their first confrontation with the limitations of the human condition.

We can never run away from what we fear; we just

take it with us. The fear draws to us the experiences we need to get to the other side of what we fear. There we find love. We fear what we love most and this fear can come out as a poison, a venom that can be injected into the wounded healer.

When performing a healing, disentangling cords, or clairvoyantly seeing into the unconscious to name a trauma, I help people to meet their deepest selves. The truth there is astounding and transformative. When a deep secret is about to be uncovered in this process, an ejection of poison, a venomous form of denial, is released. I may suffer a haziness as a web of transference is cast over me. I begin to see the unfulfilled longing of that person and his or her unloved humanity. I go deeper into the wound to reveal issues of abandonment, lack of early bonding, rejection, and the loss of self. If I persist, I see the abuses of power, and the relinquishing of power to others. Still deeper, a fear of the world, of birth, sets in. A fear of being annihilated in infancy and a fear of intimacy without fusion often emerge. Feeling pain about childhood traumas and the resulting hurt and self-punishment of early rejection and loss come out as a sting.

This scorpionic sting is an unconscious venom, a black ink, that paralyzes the psyche into despair, unfulfilled desire, and coma. Many of my patients go into temporary paralysis at this point. A total shutdown of the psyche begins as the shock seeps out as poison. This is the self-poisoning—the need to die before the real healing can begin. This is the violet bardo at its exact moment of breakthrough. The breath stops, and the person looks for the womb of the Mother. When it is not found, a substitute womb of numb detachment and coma is created.

Moments from the past are remembered and overwhelm the person when the shock rises to the surface as vague feelings and images. I begin to see cords like umbilical strings reaching out to other people for safety and to create more security by attaching to another's sense of identity or womb place. All the energy of the patient's body wants to leave at this point. I must be vigilant and stay fixed on the healing. At that moment, people die to their old selves. Nothing in their repertoire of denial and reaction to trauma works. They must invent something new. The first breaths begin when they realize that they are in illusion. There is nothing separating them from the divine except fear. I ask them not be annihilated by this union but to see a relationship with the divine as an adult grounded in the here and now. They then begin to feel their bodies and then invite the presence of love. They yearn for the divine and they receive the miracle of their healing. The divine is yearning for them more than they yearn for the divine. This is an earth-shattering experience of love, containment within the fragile self choosing to be reborn as a human being. The next step is to accept the world and its conditions, while also being sensitive to the divine and its influence. We are in a body to integrate experiences both positive and negative, which is the lesson of embracing opposites with compassion gradually over time. The timeless world and the limits of time are brought together through the workings of the human psyche.

I dispose of the poison by imagining a flame. Like a moth attracted to the flame, the poison is destroyed. A person needs to rest after this experience and let in the rebirth. This is the work of the forest acting through me, the forest which nurtured me as a child and brought me this work and teaching. As I began to accept my role as a wounded healer, I had to face everything that would sabotage that work. This was the next step.

A tree possesses a spirit. A human being possesses a soul. To give up one's freedom and right to be unique, for reasons of abandonment and grief, is to be possessed by another. To give up one's will in early childhood invites in possession. If a child has a direct contact with the unconscious but fails to create an ego base and sense of "I," feeling only a weak bond of love from parents and guardians, then subsequent adult experience may involve possession, lack of boundaries, and dominance by stronger energies inside and outside the psyche. Spirits and animals can possess shamans, but the shaman knows how to end the visitation. There are strict rules, and the shaman is in control.

To protect myself from being invaded or possessed again, I developed a positive attitude and an understanding that I had a relationship and responsibility to all the forces outside my own being. If a person is shining out or building the bridge between individuality and divinity, no outside influence can possess that psyche except for the purpose of dismemberment. To disentangle the ego, to bring humility to the human soul, a possession may occur, but only when a person is ready to be initiated into the mysteries of divinity.

We might become possessed by our visions or projections on to others, but over many incarnations these
issues return to be worked out. Past lives are important
to remember because at the next rebirth more experience
of this life can help us not to fall into the sleep of
unconsciousness again. We can create memories and
dis-create thought. In discreation, we reverse the process
of creation and disentangle ourselves from the past; this
works as long as we incorporate an essential understanding and lessons from past experience. Discreation
is a tool to erase the buildup of stressful thoughts picked
up from others during the course of the day. To cultivate
our own thoughts builds a spiritual bridge and strength.
We are all strings of light and often our particular strings
become entangled with others. This disentangling, and
deknotting of our unique light from others, is the task of
healing.

We are learning to face our illusions and use energy
properly. The correct use of energy involves seven steps:
1) having no expectations. Anything that takes us away
from the here and now drains us of energy; 2) having no
internal or external judgments or hard criticism. We
judge ourselves throughout the day, thereby losing great
amounts of energy. Every cruel thought eventually creates a sharp pain in the body; 3) changing habits.
Habitual thinking, acting, and emoting drain us of energy. We must teach the subconscious mind to be fluid; 4)
keeping death by our side. If we keep death always close
to us, we will live as if it were the last moment, and have
increased energy. The fear of death drains us of energy,
while the awareness of death spurs us to increase our

energy; 5) seeing through the body, not the eyes. Being in the heart and head and feeling the body actually improves the eyes; 6) commiting to the good fight, not reacting to people. When someone gives us the silent treatment, we do not react. In other words, we have a strategy. If we do not react, the other person will more likely see how we have changed and act accordingly. We must face the challenges of life and do not back away, but have a strategy to increase awareness; 7) cultivating non-doing. The person inside is watching whatever we do, and not reacting. This inner witness is silent knowledge, and the source of the greatest strength.

With energy, I have found an empowerment in emptiness that is indescribable. Each purification brings me closer to accepting union with the divine, and individuality at the same time. Intention is the key to magic and to awareness. Intention taught me that only with enough energy can we transcend our destiny.

PART FOUR

Facing the Lesser
and
Greater Guardians

CHAPTER 14

Eleusinian Mysteries

In 1996, I began to have vivid images of climbing trees and sitting high atop their branches to commune with the tree spirit. I took walks in the Santa Fe and Pecos national forests in New Mexico, and began to have memories of an earlier life in Greece during the time of the Eleusinian Mysteries. I was conscious of knowing what had happened in Greece for two thousand years and that I had been spiritually opened in an earlier time. I will give an account of each day of a pilgrimage to honor the Goddess Demeter. There I began to see connections between my experience of the centaur Chiron and the rites of Eleusis.

According to Greek mythology, Chiron lived in a cave on the north side of Mount Pelion, overlooking the valley of Pelethronion. In shamanism, north is the direction of the teacher, the wise person, the one who endures the trials of death to find the self and who is then a link to other worlds. Chiron's healing is to synthesize the animal and the human. His is the journey to the depths of inner nature, to the abandoned father and mother, to become the horse bridled. This is instinct disciplined, an education into a world of herbs and plants that induce visions, and the birth of a deeper consciousness.

At the foot of Mount Pelion, near where Chiron lived, is Lake Boibeis. The goddess of this lake is Persephone;

she is the daughter of the goddess Demeter. Persephone is said to have given birth at this lake to a new being, a child named Brimos, representing a new consciousness. Demeter, the "mare-headed" goddess, is linked to Chiron and embodies his opposite. Her horse head is the union of the mental realm with instinct, and her human body has instinct suffused with intelligence.

Demeter is called the Black One when in the guise of the mare-headed goddess. She reminds me of the Black Madonnas seen in churches throughout Europe. In Greece, she is the Black Horse Mother. She taught Chiron her mysteries and her experiments with plant substances and herbs.

Chiron, like Demeter, is heralding the death of one way of living to the birth of a new marriage of instinct, inner nature, reason, and education. As the wounded healer, he sees the top of the mountain as well as the valley's depth, and is poised between them as the teacher of a new way of being in balance. We must be in control of our instincts to acknowledge the divine and accept the values of family, intimacy, companionship, and community.

Demeter, her daughter Persephone, and the birth of the divine child—a future consciousness—are the focal points of the Eleusinian Mysteries. The *kykos*, a special drink taken by the initiates, may be a plant substance that creates visions similar to those of ayahuasca. Here, we enter the world of shamanic cultures, an initiation into other realities that give meaning to our present lives.

In Greece the Mysteries of Eleusis and their rituals lasted for sixteen hundred years. Their origin is traced to the second half of the fifteenth century B.C. Initiates would pass through the gates of the telesterion into a dimly lit chamber—a sanctuary for the mysteries of life. Men, women, children, both freeman and slaves, embarked on the journey. The Mysteries—open to all— rich or poor, Greek or non-Greek—were rituals to bring the submerged maiden back from the Underworld.

The myth of Persephone, also called Kore, and her mother, was an integral part of the Mysteries. Demeter was the mother goddess, who had lost her daughter to Pluto in a rape. Persephone lost her innocence and was carried forcefully to the Underworld by Pluto, forced to be Pluto's wife, submerged in the densest matter. She had to purify herself through her suffering to find innate wisdom in the depths of her psyche. Demeter, the goddess of grain and the art of agriculture, threatened the world with famine if her daughter was not returned to her. She finally struck a bargain by which her daughter would be returned from the Underworld, where she was queen, from spring through summer each year. In the fall and winter, like the seed, she was returned to her husband inside the belly of the earth.

For me, the Mysteries also relate to the Gnostic myths of Sophia and Lucifer in the Western Mystery Tradition. Sophia was the trapped woman of wisdom, the soul in all of us. Lucifer was a creator of human beings who entrapped humanity in time. The Eleusinian Mysteries were an attempt to release, in all of us, the bondage of Sophia's wisdom and passion for higher expression after the fall from grace. Through facing their own accumulated karma, participants would meet the

Virgin Sophia or Persephone, allowing their souls to have their freedom. In Greece, this ritual release was activated through a nine-day celebration of facing the Guardians of the Threshold, a term used in the Western Mystery Tradition that may have been borrowed from Eleusis.

From the autumn equinox to October first, the Archon of the ceremonies, acting as a guide and hierophant for the participants, protected the group by invoking the intercession of a deity that strongly resembles Archangel Michael. "Michael" gave the facilitators of the rituals an infusion of spiritual understanding and knowledge of other worlds. This was done through the Muses, through the imaginative merging of consciousness between the initiates and the spiritual or "supersensible worlds" (as the Western Mystery Tradition calls them). At the time of ancient Greece, we had not evolved as a species to the point of true individuality in the spiritual worlds, and therefore we had to ingest plant substances to have visions and be in a dreamlike state. We were "inspired" by the gods instead of acquiring the answers from within ourselves.

This is another crucial difference between the Eleusinian rites and today. Between the twelfth and fourteenth centuries, human beings became an "I" consciousness, individualized, with a distinct ego that could recall their innate cosmic memory without being overshadowed by a Hieroceryx (a hierophant) in Mystery Schools. We could go inside, to the developing Christ or solar consciousness within our souls, and find the energy to be clairvoyant. We had lost this ability after

Atlantean times, when the pineal gland was on the top of the head and spiritual awareness was much more comprehensive. The pineal gland retracted and shriveled into a pea-sized organ inside the middle and lower brain. It was more difficult after the destruction of Atlantis to remember our origin and our gifts from God.

Memory continues to reside in the magnetic fields of Earth. After the last catastrophe in Atlantis, where almost sixty million souls died suddenly, the magnetic poles shifted and an ice age resulted. Ancient Atlantean souls forgot their past, in a cultural amnesia, because of the shift in magnetic fields. Although our deepest memories of the ancient past have been forgotten, they still exist in the pineal gland which is less affected by magnetic pole reversals. We have to loosen the pineal gland to cosmically perceive once again, and to develop our brain potential.

The Western Mystery Tradition describes both an Old Moon way of seeing that involves "inspired," "channeled," or psychic contact, and a newer way of having clairvoyant sight and perceiving other realms directly. We are awakening and being reborn on the other side of the spiritual curtain with a new maturity. There has been an iron curtain between the material and the supersensible worlds. As that boundary begins to drop at this turn of the century, the supersensible world will draw out our lies, self-deceptions, destructive karmas, and withholdings from others, our most hidden secrets and our fears of the unknown. We will collectively and consciously enter a kind of bardo or Purgatory. The Last Judgment is the mirroring of our selves, in all our existences, to perceive our totality, blemishes and all. If we refuse to face our emotional, lower astral bodies, we will be either possessed or create more negative karma.

We are clearing our memories by reliving the myths of the past in our everyday lives. The first purification is the replaying in childhood of the story of Adam and Eve. A child feels in the bliss of the womb—the Garden—the forbidden fruit of consciousness offered by the serpent and the subsequent expulsion from the Mother's Paradise at birth. Bodily shame and suffering from the separation from the womb, as if the mother and child have a wall between them, is the result. Almost every serious illness in life stems from this perceived original break. In the future, the people who discreate this myth will be better able to take up the burden and happiness of an individual life.

As we clear the wounds of childhood, the Eleusinian Mysteries lead us to a new area of discovery. One aspect of this initiation is the formation of a healthy ego, which is the gatekeeper to the greater Self; this ego is synonymous with the Lesser Guardian in the Western Mystery Tradition. We will all face this challenge as a species during the coming millennium. The ego tests us to see if we are ready to let go of the past and accept the responsibility of our humanity.

The following is my recall of the mystery school rituals that occurred in ancient Greece. These visions came to me during walks in the forests near my home in Santa Fe, New Mexico.

I entered the Mysteries in the agora or marketplace,

the place of karma and worldly involvement. As a participant I was taught to observe the marketplace of material goods with detachment and to question what was truly of value in life. What are love, relationship, honesty, caring, and are they priorities in commonplace life? In addition, the concept of karma was illustrated through what had to be paid for and what didn't.

On the second day, I followed a procession to a ritual bath in the sea for purification. The word Eleusis comes from a word meaning "to cleanse" or "to loosen." Eleusis was situated near the sea and its currents. Purification of the chakras and of the physical, astral, and etheric bodies was essential. The "loosening" involved opening the pineal gland for intelligent cognition of the symbols and the mysteries and for cosmic memory of the past—for wisdom and to learn from mistakes. The sea is the place of our origins, the fluid of the womb, and we are fish that have adapted to the land from the great sea of consciousness.

Up to this point, I was detached on my pilgrimage, and then suddenly I experienced the taste of the pineal opening, and my ears began to whistle, and a whole new perception opened to me. I was still in this world, but all my senses were heightened, and I could feel huge rushes of vibrant energy up my spine and shooting out the top of my head with dizzying colors. I perceived that in ancient times, as we were evolving into human beings, there was an opening at the top of our heads and at the base of our spines for a different kind of breathing. I had to breathe up my spine in a circular breath, like a dolphin or whale, to open the passage at the base and at the top of my head. This form of breathing was very liberating, and the space between breaths was filled with a kind of spiritual or etheric energy. The pause between breaths, or the empty space between the joints, is all etheric energy and is more powerful than material bone and tissue. I saw how the body is created by the consciousness and how every cell is replaced every two years. I could see how thoughts can change our bodies, expanding into the physical gaps and empty spaces within us. I saw the pure spiritual substance, like a light, at the center of the bones in my body. I was beginning to shine from within and was finally ready to continue.

At the end of the second and the third day of the Mysteries, the animal nature was sacrificed, a sacrifice of certain base instincts and a clearing of the lower animal chakras of survival. Animals were seen as representing emotional aspects of human beings frozen in matter, hardened by being too attached to the physical world. Each animal symbolized a different emotional state. In Eleusis, I had to face my animal soul. I dreamt of a special wild bull sacrificed to the gods. All my stubbornness and resistance had to be sacrificed, leaving both a greater emptiness and a greater strength. At Knossos in Crete, in the court of King Minos, women and men would perform acrobatics on the backs of bulls.

The Greater Mysteries (Eleusinia) were preceded in the spring by the Lesser Mysteries (Antheria). In the Lesser Mysteries, I had to close my senses down completely. I was lowered into the water of the river Ilissus until I completely stopped breathing. I could view more clearly my entire etheric body and its memories when my

brain was deprived of oxygen. Like a near-death experience, it forced me to loosen my etheric and astral bodies
from the physical, which literally loosened and slipped
off me like taking off a coat. In the moment of stillness
before total death by drowning, I was prepared to see and
to recapitulate my entire life. I witnessed events in more
than one dimension, as if on a movie screen, feeling my
actions and the responses of others to the emotional
events of my life. I experienced leaving my body and
holding on to a cord as I drifted into the sky and looked
down at the events of my life like an eagle. The pictures
showed noncompletions with other people in this life and
the history of my soul before this incarnation. At the precise moment before actual death by drowning, I was lifted out of the water and brought back to life with a strong
slap to the back of the neck—to force the etheric body
back in place. Adepts were trained to clairvoyantly know
the exact moment to bring the bodies back. My soul was
returned from its life review and was ready to go beyond
self-delusion to proper initiation. I could feel a great deal
of love, forgiveness, and warmth from this experience,
and I felt protected by a great light.

The fourth day was dedicated to the god Asclepias,
the son of Apollo, and the healer taught by Chiron in his
cave. Asclepias helped heal the previous incarnations of
the soul through a kind of cosmic review going back millions of years. Ancestral memory was awakened or called
up from the soul. This was a time to purge curses and
release attached spirits. The initiates on either side of me
learned cosmic history and its personal relationship to
their evolution as a soul. That night, we went home to

contemplate what we had learned. In my dreams, my pineal gland was activated to produce vivid views of other cycles in history. Besides a kind of etheric inward review, I saw an exoteric review of Atlantis, Lemuria, and two earlier civilzations, and then the creation of the world. I distinctly remember speaking with animals and to nature and becoming a series of animals and trees. I knew that animals in the far past could speak to human beings and were our teachers.

On the fifth day, or *pompe* which means departure, I was among a group of people, crowned in myrtle leaves, who were led through a double gate after a fourteen-mile trek. This gate was called "Dipylon." One side was for the Lesser Guardian of Death, and the other was for the Greater Guardian or Higher Self. Led by a donkey, we walked in through the gate from the northwest after passing hills, the sacred fig tree, a shrine to Aphrodite, a statue of Jacchus, and a narrow bridge. A saffron-colored ribbon was tied to my right hand and left leg as I crossed to the Gate of Death with hundreds of other souls. The bridge was the symbolic crossing from the known material world to the Unknown sanctuary.

Insults and jeerings accompanied those who crossed over the bridge; facing the ego was important at this point. Obscenities and accusations were hurled at me and the other initiates—hardly the behavior one would expect from an audience of their peers. This kept each of us humble, teasing us in order to face our own insecurities (which have sabotaged me most of my life through self-abnegation or inflated feelings of self-importance. I had to shatter my self-important image to know the divine). I endured the barrage of insults in Eleusis and entered the *temenos*, the sanctuary of Demeter and Persephone. This was a great honor.

On the sixth day, the fast was broken and the sacred chalices called the "Kernoe,"—similar to the Holy Grail— were brought into the "wedding chamber." As an initiate, I identified my will, intellect, and emotions. The intellect or mental part of myself was becoming awake; the emotional or astral body was asleep and had to begin lucid dreaming; my will had not been sufficiently used and had to be engaged. These three parts of the psyche were continually tested and reviewed and were always distinct.

The ego was represented as a physical gatekeeper, a man with a mask, to taunt, chide, and act out the karma that manifested throughout my life on Earth. He stood before me like a mirror. Through trance, I actually saw my selfishness, ruthlessness, and lower astral self in a hall of mirrors and projections. Every part of my shadow was manifested in front of me. I fought my own image and stripped myself at one point. I wanted to run away or hide, but the gatekeeper looked into my eyes and brought me through a deep feeling of childhood fear. It was irrational fear. The gatekeeper then clothed my head and laid me down to die. This was a ritual death to the old self, but I felt that I was leaving my body. I had to let go of Dawn Eagle Woman in that moment. She had been my teacher up to this time, but now she and I had to move away from each other. She had mothered me and guided my spiritual growth, but now was no longer needed and could in fact be detrimental to my future growth. I saw that if our relationship continued, I would feel undermined because I had learned what I needed to learn from her. I only wanted her approval now; and on my spiritual journey to realize God, I had to stop looking outside myself for approval from others. Finally, the gatekeeper cut off the remains of my lower astral body with a ritual knife. I sacrificed my habitual passions and unhealthy miasms in the unconscious. I was cut from my old connection to Dawn Eagle Woman and would not contact her again for a long time. I felt considerably lighter and more serene.

The gatekeeper had seen my lower astral body connected through a cord to my navel and cut it precisely. All emotional cords to my past teachers had to be cut and all cords to my family, friends, lovers, as if I were no longer a child needing an umbilical cord to survive in the world. I was feeling unencumbered as the cords were broken one by one, and bright colors soothed and repaired the holes left by them. I was in a kind of psychic surgery with sealing threads closing up old wounds, attachments, and dependencies that I had finally outgrown.

At this point Demeter, or Sophia as the Great Mother, was allowed to enter. After my lower astral body was cut off and sufficiently dispensed with, I could perceive her face. The cutting was a shock, as the ritual knife destroyed the connection to the past emotional illusions of human life. Only the deeper, higher emotions of real love remained. My senses were closed down so as to not interfere with the releasing. The Great Mother was before me, and I stopped feeling terrified from the cutting or afraid of the next step.

As every initiate must do, I asked Persephone to enter

my body. She lived in matter as Sophia, the Great Mother and creator of elemental life, who created the air, water, fire, and earth, and the etheric separations—called the "Pleroma"—from the first world beyond time and space. She had fallen from an exalted world because of her desire to be passionate, to learn again, and to give of her wisdom in a passionate way. She was labeled *maya* or ignorance for her need to be conscious of right and wrong, and her need to find fulfillment and instill that in us. She became the maiden Persephone or Virgin Sophia, the Logos of wisdom, our desire to see the sacred in the commonplace and the divine in the material world. To know her in Eleusis, I had to destroy the lower Sophia, her base passions of ignorance, greed, impatience, destruction, and wrath, and perceive her as whole—encompassing both light and dark in balance. I had to restore her innocence—the passionate, free, and clear feminine soul. She was our collective soul trapped in matter, wanting to experience the divine from whence it came.

The mystae brought Sophia, like Persephone, from the bowels of Earth, from exile in dense matter to the light of consciousness. I let Sophia initiate and guide me to face the Greater Guardian. There, I let go of all concepts, ideas, feelings about other worlds. I divested myself of expectations. I felt realized in a higher perception and completely empty. My mind entered the mysteries of nature, and corn plants were placed in my hands with seeds, and the pictures of pure light formed in front of me. I began to experience God through the language of number, proportion, and geometry. I witnessed the creation of the world like an embryogenesis, a cellular mitosis, the evolution of my chromosomes and how they develop certain brain capacities. I saw the Platonic solids, the tetrahedrons of fire forming above and below me, turning and intersecting at the midpoint of my heart. I could see the *vesica piscis* and a series of circles clustering in specific elemental patterns, the building blocks of life, like a huge lotus pattern. Through geometry, I began to experience a wave length of light coming toward me, going through my cells. With it I would be able to create perfect health and reverse diseases. Illness is a way to learn on Earth, to learn lessons and to grow through suffering and healing, but it will not be an important form of learning in the future. The science of wave length and, to a lesser degree, the frequency of sound will be the keys to ending disease in the twenty-first century. My perception was that illness must end so that more time can be spent in spiritual development.

Next, we each gave Demeter or Sophia permission to enter the gateway for us. She was our surrogate. I faced a large gateway, and I motioned for her to walk before me. She was shining, and I was bowing to her presence and mystery. She was initiated, returning to her original position as the Holy Spirit or Goddess of Spirit in our place. That was the moment of surrender to Her. I saw her in an incredible light, a radiance that was transfixing. I saw her as Demeter and Persephone, but I knew she was Black Isis, Mother Mary, the goddess Kali in India. I saw that all women are goddesses and all goddesses are One. I saw that Persephone had convulsions, like an epileptic. She needed to learn how to open her pineal gland. We were initiating this mystery for her. She would be free to join the light of spring and summer and illumine the everyday world with wisdom, truth, and beauty. Through us and our honoring, she became transparent.

Next came her sacred wedding to the Christed One. Her consort was the Christ in the form of Dionysius. I knew he was the Sun King, Ram in India, and Osiris in Egypt. He was the one who would shed blood as a fully realized divine embodiment of the Logos. He was the gods awakened to full potential in the flesh. He made love to and ravished Sophia in a sacred marriage ceremony. We all witnessed these events and felt the serpent of kundalini rise up our spines as the air was charged with their consummation. I felt my own instincts and higher mind fuse together in their sexual union. I could feel the gods and humans uniting to birth a son and a daughter, ancestors of humanity.

In a kind of sacrament, all the initiates, including myself, drank water mixed with barley and mint, which also contained a plant substance that helped us have a clear, cognitive vision of the proceedings. We felt more awake in an exalted state outside of time, and we saw everything from a heightened eaglelike perspective. We walked in long processions in precise steps, watching our breath, and entering into other dimensions and experiences of people and places that were not physically present in the room.

At the conclusion of the ceremonies, advanced students from previous visits to Eleusis were given further instructions. Advanced schooling about the other side of the veil was given with conscious cognition of other worlds. I entered into a new world of weaving pictures. That is the only way I can explain it—my vision was altered to perceive many dimensions at once. The Mysteries entered my physical body and reawakened in me in the late twentieth century. That teaching and powerful crowned force of truth prepared me for this transformation of matter to spirit and feeling.

Eleusis is an introduction to the facing of the Lesser Guardian and the Greater Guardian in the Western Mystery Tradition. It is time for all of us to participate consciously again in these Mysteries, in our present bodies while alive.

Themistius of Paphlagonia gives an insight into the process: "The [dying] soul has the same experience as those who are being initiated into the greater mysteries . . . at first one wanders and wearily hurries to and fro, and journeys with suspicion through the dark as one uninitiated; then come all the terrors, trembling, sweating, amazement: then one is struck with marvelous light, one is received into pure regions and meadows, with voices and dances and majesty of holy sounds and shapes: among these the one who fulfilled initiation wanders free, and released and bearing his/her crown joins in the divine communion, and consorts with pure and holy men [and women]. . . ."[1]

CHAPTER 15

Meeting the Guardians and the Gateway

To shamanically midwife a whole culture at the beginning of the twenty-first century, we must first realize that we are entering the age of Sophia, a newer form of the mare-headed Demeter, an updating of Eleusinian Mysteries, a time of the Goddess, and we must enter a new partnership with her. The feminine understanding of God and our origins in the water of mare, mater, mother, and our rebirth to the land and the forest are the future progression of initiation into the divine.

We all must be immersed in a purplish "wine dark" sea to finally find the waters of life and walk on the land through the two trees, the gateway to the inner realm of balance. Sophia is our first guide to the voices of the Violet Forest. In initiatory schools, Sophia was called the Achamod, or Lower Sophia. She is the elemental world of air, fire, earth, and water. She is emotional, a bit clouded in her exile from the Pleroma. She is our passions for the material world. I love her in a strong way and see her in me. She is in my emotional, astral body, and is the Old Moon in me. She wanted me to undertake an alchemical purification.

The first stage began with meditation, concentration, emotional release, and cathartic work, having a clear understanding of the chakra system in the body with the constant cleaning of cognition. She wanted me to develop etheric imagination and imagine how I could re-create the material world through direct perception of reality. To open the etheric, I had to concentrate on the spaces between breaths, the spaces between my joints, and mediate on the Void and great emptiness.

Sophia is Wisdom, and in her Virgin aspect she could prepare me for purifying my astral, emotional body. To heal and understand our own character helps us to know wisdom. A great deal of inner work is needed, in addition to work in the world, to gain a little cultivated wisdom. The more we truly work on ourselves and the shadow, the more clear and precise the wisdom.

The inner psyche must be mastered gradually because the lower nature will be separated from the higher nature. This is a dangerous period that most psychics, mediums, and counselors must face. Their own natures run rampant because thinking, feeling, willing, intuiting, and sensing are all independent entities with their own will. If not sufficiently disciplined, they can find themselves going in many different directions. This can lead to strange personality traits and negative behaviors. Many people including myself have been quite unbearable at this stage! The worst in us erupts suddenly. We run amuck. We have great fantasies, wild images, which lead to inflation and contraction in equal amounts. We are alone, and our inner life is an uprising!

At this point, we then need to fill our imagination with warmth, kindness, patience, and real love. I had to develop an iron will over time to have the courage to face myself and to voluntarily suffer. I had to confront how my mother's suffering became my own by osmosis. As a child, I was identified with my mother's neediness. I saw her disappointments, and I had to separate from her to achieve something in my own life. This is what initially drew me into the healing profession. I did not want a sacrificial life. Identification with the archetypal realities of Sophia, Lucifer, and Ahriman bring a great deal of power. Yet this power is borrowed, it is not earned, especially if we try to use it to compensate for what was lacking in our early life. I had to go back to my birth and find a balance with myself, to find my own power base. It takes a lot of discipline, various purifications, and cleansing of the chakras to have the power to clairvoyantly see on our own.

I have always felt my thinking was active, and my feelings as well, not only in dreams, and I have finally found my will. In reality, most of us are dreaming our feelings and the will is absent. I wanted to be free to act and to see the consequences of those actions karmically. Most persons are asleep and are catalyzed to act out of necessity, compulsion, force. We can learn to will our thoughts and gain mastery.

Recapitulation, the review of the events of our lives, can help in this process. We make an inquiry from our birth into everything we can discover about ourselves. We go over every relationship, every exchange of energy from the present to our conception. We create soul pictures with color and forms and sounds. This is our etheric body in time. We see into the mirror, and it takes a long time to look back at everything presented.

The images always change, infusing the past with

new forms, organic in nature, not spatial or particularly linear. We learn to think freely. Our review brings us face-to-face with the great being in our soul. Then we must let it go and rid ourselves of it. In its place comes a new consciousness that is very aware.

In the recapitulation, I saw events in my life from many perspectives. I had to review every second of my life from now back to birth. In a black box, I had to re-see and re-direct all the energies of my childhood and from every relationship in my life. The energy from every emotional exchange began to return to me as the past was erased. I saw it all as a sense perception, amazing, but then had to finally depart. Thoughts are elemental beings, shadows of another world. Spiritual beings are mental pictures. We can learn eventually to have our own thoughts. I learned to banish thoughts by scrutinizing them with a deep stare. If through intense staring at the image, it dissolves and never comes back, then it is not real. If I stare at it and it dissolves, then if it re-creates itself and is persistent, it is a fact. When I view the Akashic Records or records of the soul existence through many incarnations, I test what I perceive by banishing certain images, and the ones that return exactly in the same form are real.

Sophia wants the fullness of her being. She wants us to be fully aware for her. The passion of her banishment created the world we inhabit. We are helping her to return home with every discernment and awareness of clarity.

Next, the astral body has to go through a purification to become pure feeling. It is emptied of its past karmic accumulations and is cut off with a sword of discernment. It is a great letting go. The Virgin Sophia now feels she can come forward and make herself known. She illumines us, and the forms and seeing of the astral body are given to the etheric body. We are given a living weaving of thought which can be interpreted. We then meet the shadow, called the Guardian of the Threshold, the real gatekeeper in ourselves. Next we meet the spirits behind the elements, such as fairies, elves, gnomes, undines, sylphs, and salamanders. We see their relationship to us and our own imagination. Through animation of the world, we meet a world of thought-forms and spirits like ancient animists. We can then go through a dark night of the soul to the Midnight Sun. We enter the darkness to meet the spiritual presences in the Sun. We have entered the other world. We begin to watch the motions of planets and stars and inward space.

When I began this initiation, I had to face a beast. The lion of my egotism and will was free and raging. The lion wanted to kill me. I had to take its mouth, like a charioteer must take the firm reins of a black and white horse and keep the balance. In the Tarot, you open the lion's mouth with your bare hands. I faced tremendous terror. The lion started to open my chakras; I was learning to control the lion within, to have strength.

After this bout, another beast came, one that raises its head in workshops, in projections of participants—the dragon. I had to first learn to see the dragon and look it in the eyes. If we do not see the beast, we may be in illusion. I saw how in the past, I had channeled images from my own digestion and belly. I thought with my belly.

Elementals from food in my organs and digestion were this dragon. I faced the dragon of pride, avarice, lust, vanity, self-seeking, and immersion. The basest instincts came out ferociously and were ugly to see. I am that crazy, wild dragon who had to leave behind the need to merge with everything in pursuit of bliss. I had to let go of the anxiety for attaining spiritual heights. I saw that my instincts and sexuality wanted me to continue to evolve by facing my negativity. When I accepted the dragon, I felt more human.

The passing of the initiation is to see the dragon as ourselves. Inner recognition and acceptance are the dragon-slayer. From the dragon and lion and the initiation into death comes the emerging Sophia. She is our purified astral body. The astral body before this was instinctual, passionate, and filled with selfishness. I had lived for too long in the dreams of other beings from an ancient Lemurian time. Earlier I was a copy of their spiritual thoughts and feelings, but they were just dreams, images, the fake surrogate. This had to do with creation; I was being acted upon by a higher being, but was not yet independent. I no longer wanted to be an instrument of the gods. Archangel Michael wanted me to be an "I," to be aware, and this was the course of my evolution.

Next we must approach the Guardian of the Threshold, which some call the Higher Self, but for me the image was Chiron, the consummate teacher of sacrifice and healing. Chiron brought me to a door made from two trees. I instantly knew that this was the Violet Forest, the entry into the world of union with opposites. The other world beyond the veil is sealed shut, like a closed door blocks easy human access. The world beyond is subtle, a formative world of celestial beings. Not everyone would be able to face the immensity of this world and its overwhelming nature. We fear this Void, and the ego holds us back. We fear how devastating and destructive it could be. Here, I faced the blind rage of my own inner being.

In esoteric science there are two Guardians, the one who is Lesser and the one who is Greater. The Lesser guards the inner door, and for me this was mare-headed Demeter, the ancient Horse Woman, a potent shamanic symbol. The Greater, symbolized by Chiron, was the master of instinct and intellect who guards the outer door. He is our ego masked. The Lesser Guardian comes as our own weakness and shame. This Guardian is our nightly dream contents and unclarified passions, the unintegrated shadow. Everything we have rejected in ourselves becomes our mirror.

When I realized the Lesser Guardian was my initiator and my own self-projections, I began to speak with it. Sometimes it can come as a pack of wild dogs or a large shadow, but I realized this was my ego, the accumulation of lifetimes of unconsciousness, neglect, and karma. The Guardian came with a mare-headed face and I recognized her as Demeter, she who taught me discernment and how to be genuine. Through discrimination, I discerned what were my own self-projections and what were cosmic realities. I had to pass through imagination, intuition, and inspiration, and proceed to a deeper inner schooling.

The Guardian helped me to see myself as I truly am

and to begin the real work of soul. My astral and etheric bodies separated from my physical body and became looser and more free to be autonomous. Their independence prefigured my own. I had to face in my astral body the total desires and passions of all my lives on Earth. Then I saw the demons, my own accumulated astral energy. I faced those unresolved parts to get through all my deceptions and see the full contents of my psyche. I met the "personalities" in myself. I also saw how little progress I had made in other lives. I felt humbled and was paralyzed for a time.

If we can face and see ourselves honestly with the Lesser Guardian, we then face the shining presence of what many call the Higher Self or Greater Guardian, who is transformed into Chiron, the master teacher. He is a light being who holds real knowledge of the Self. He knows us intimately. He holds this knowledge, to safeguard it until we are prepared to protect ourselves and face the Void, where we must each still be an "I," or we will lose everything. The Greater Guardian prevents this premature surrender. With the Lesser Guardian, we face time, our past. With the Greater Guardian, we face space. The cosmos is an expansion of the "I" consciousness. We are the compression of the cosmos.

The first thing that we see when we cross over the threshold is both Guardians. Then we see our double. We see our new-born self. The Greater Guardian takes off its mask and is the radiant Christ, whom we are becoming. When we successfully make this passage, we see the Christ face-to-face. He is the spirit of human beings, its ideal form. Many Buddhists have seen Buddha at this point, Yogis see Shiva, but my experience was of Christ.

The dual-faced Guardian, the ego, is always what we see first. This transforms into the Higher Self. Then it evolves into Chiron or the Christ-permeated ego, the "I am" Self. We stand on the threshold as Sophia. We become the Virgin. We enter a new land, a vista of the supersensible world. Through the purified astral body, our organs of perception are clearer. We see Sophia as the bride of Christ. We are clean of sense-bound concepts, and she emerges from the inner alchemy. She crosses the threshold for us. Through infused imagination, with the force of Sophia, we enter awake into the spiritual. The development of these higher organs of perception liberates spiritual energy for seeing. Our thoughts create pictures that are alive, leading us into spiritual freedom and the development of true free will and wakeful cognition.

We end our own dreamy, group-soul clairvoyance and enter the active etheric world, eyes open. This is a revolution in consciousness. All the mysteries are now being revealed to an entire culture about to embark on matriarchal revelation.

Hummingbird Medicine and the Transformation of the Moon

After these initiations, Chiron told me, "Now that the wild horse in you has been faced and I am free, your suffering can end and a joy fill you like the hummingbird. From facing the mare-headed Mother, and finding me, the teacher inside, you now can face your indomitable spirit, the hummingbird. These are the symbols of wakening to enlightenment for the future. They are borne of the Violet Forest and are the essence of the teachings of the trees."

In meditation, I see the smooth surface of the water. If I throw in a stone, the surface changes, and the surface of this world changes. Life is impermanence, reverberation, the shadow of another divine world. The surface of this world is illusory, mutable. My practice is to throw a stone in that water and that stone is Hummingbird Medicine.

To break the mirror of the ego, I ask myself fundamental questions. Who am I? What is the nature of life? What are the origins of being truly human? What is real? What do I really desire? What does the emptiness of desire feel like? Hummingbird Medicine questions everything and, with a loving balanced eye, brings us to the joy of the cosmos. It has no system, no formula for success, and no religion. It is the questioning of Spirit and soul and "I consciousness" to know love.

What is essential to living a full life? The simplicity of practicing what we say, the simplicity of discerning what is honest. Self-examination by a group of peers, not "yes" people, keeps us inquisitive and honest. Personal self-examination keeps us less prone to violence and dishonesty and allows us to be free. Hummingbird Medicine enables an individual or a group to do self-inquiry without narcissism or nihilism and therefore without judgment. We can see ourselves as we are, love and accept those selves, and gradually embrace the love in another.

Hummingbird Medicine prepares a person for death and immortality. Nothing dies; it is forever free and universal. Energy is never destroyed. The spirit of a tree is in the acorn. The spirit of a human being is the acorn of the soul, which is indestructible as it witnesses the mystery of all things. The Holy Spirit cannot be annihilated and neither can reality. A hummingbird drinks nectar from a flower. The word nectar comes from the Greek *nekros* meaning death. The hummingbird drinks the elixir of death to create resurrection. We all must die and go through the initiation at the door of death while still alive to face the astral body and the Lesser Guardian of the Threshold. Chiron is the initiator at the door of death because he sacrificed his own immortality to free the Promethean spirit in us all.

The hummingbird follows lunar cycles, specifically the influx of the waning Moon, to distill the nectar that stimulates our brains to produce neuro-secretions of full awakening. From drinking the elixir of death, the hummingbird extracts the ancient elixir of immortality.

The hummingbird achieves its goal and has meaning in terms of the awakening of humanity to the other world. Hummingbird Medicine dislikes systems, and cosmologies, and is worthy of inquiry. It is the joy of new etheric and light body experiences through investigation and story, word, sound, awareness.

I know that actual hummingbirds may have been humans in previous lives. They could have been warriors fixated on the material, and have now found the real bliss, before incarnating as human beings again. The hummingbird has the largest heart for its body size of any animal, and is the only bird that can fly backward. It seems to remain suspended in the air while it drinks its rapturous nectar.

I fixed my heart on one point, and the hummingbird inside the warrior in me opened that heart. May your heart open and may nothing seem impossible to you. There is a time to read books, to be challenged by new insights and stories of the soul, and there is a time to put books away. Life is right timing or synchronous timing. At the right moment, when you have prepared yourself to receive the elixir, may a hummingbird enter your home through a window or a door and may you want to enter beyond the veil to another world of weaving pictures.

The hummingbird might interrupt your work, your painting, or your meal, and announce itself like the Guardian of the Threshold. A hummingbird might hit itself against the window glass and need you to hold it in its state of torpor. The bird might rest on your hands and share its life energy with you. This is the beginning of the call to awakening, when the hummingbird opens the home of your heart and there is no turning back.

The hummingbird is a material embodiment of the emotion joy, and it awakens joy in our dense bodies. This bird hums like the etheric body, like the sound of the swirling etheric encasement or sheath. It reminds us of what is beyond this world, in the next, and therefore is a psychopomp or guide to the supersensible. At night, the hummingbird enters into a state of death, called torpor, closing down its perception and retreating into a violet darkness only to resurrect itself in the morning. All mystery schools were preparations for dying as when the breath was slowed as in yogic practices. The perception of the inner body is found in the heart, the heart focuses on a point, and the body slows down to integrate the nectar of life. We can slow down, gather ourselves, find what is of value, and receive the sweetness of life.

The flower can be seen as the lotus of the chakras. Through pollination, it carries the essences of flowers, of imagination, as we can accomplish beyond the veil. The hummingbird opens the channels of sensitivity in us to see the Age of Flowers, and it extracts the nectar from our own chakras. These are the deeper understandings and our own one-pointed directness. This nectar is transformed through attention into an elixir. This is the essence of Hummingbird Medicine.

Patanjali, in his exquisite *Yoga Sutras*, describes Hummingbird Medicine. He talks of *dharan*—concentration, absorption in the object you are contemplating— such as the hummingbird's relationship to the flower. In the second stage is *dhyana* or contemplation and mindfulness. I call this the hummingbird-waiting-on-the-tree-branch alert. It must know and listen to its own body process thoroughly, and perceive its surroundings, and still be one-pointed in its pursuit of nectar. The third stage is *samadhi*, when the hummingbird voluntarily goes into a state of death at night for regeneration and total assimilation of the elixir. The last stage is *samyama* and the attainment of *kaivalya*, when the heart of the hummingbird is no longer a distraction and the senses are stilled. When the hummingbird physically dies, its liberation becomes a part of everything and its consciousness lives on and can guide us to freedom through the joy found in awareness and perseverance on the spiritual path of the soul. These are the stages of immortality.

The ancient Vedic term for the essence of the waning Moon is "Soma." The Persian term is *haoma*. The elixir of immortality has always been associated with Moon cycles. The hummingbird is aware of the Moon and that its cycles affect both us and the bird. Indra, the king of the gods in the Vedic hymns, had soma in the belly as in the fetus. We listen to find the Great Mother in the belly and the elixir she provides. Indra has strength in the body and wisdom in the head and lightning in his hands.

William Blake wrote about Albion, the giant inside the Earth. Together, we as a species are still just being born to wakeful "I" consciousness. We learn of Albion's existence slowly, but we are consciously awaiting birth. Earth is our collective womb, that we create through pictures, sounds, and imaginings. Christ and Michael help us to birth enlightened, aware human beings out of incubation. That is the purpose of Hummingbird Medicine in the Age of Flowers.

We can extract the nectar of life, the imaginings of flowers and learn to see in a new conscious way the world and our co-creation of it as human beings. We live in an etheric envelope that is sexual, biological. In sexual orgasm, we often feel deeply close to God, the energies beyond the veil. Organic life feeds off this energy, and our etheric light bodies are created from this life force. (Wilhelm Reich called it orgone. Orgone accumulators are said to make warmth in a vacuum.) Again, the etheric light body is a source of warmth for human beings. Compassion is a process of moving from the astral passions to genuine warmth. Energy is drawn up the spine into the brain and down through the root or sexual chakra as a cycle. These are the principles of Taoism and certain tantric schools, reflecting the patterns of the waxing and waning Moon cycles.

As the hummingbird works with lunar cycles, it is creating orgone, not dissipating its energy. The hummingbird's efficiency coheres with lunar cycles to stimulate the secretions of hormones in our brains. Through mindfulness, refinement, and distillation, certain hormones can regenerate the body and help in the creation of a spiritual light body.

When this energy rises up to the hypothalamus and pituitary gland, it releases an elixir from the hormones that gradually transforms the physical body into a spiritual body. Spirituality is latent, premeditated in form. The Logos is inside form waiting to be made awake. The large cosmic Albion wishes to wake up inside of us and walk. The outcome is for our souls, through Sophia, to return home from the Old Moon consciousness to the new

Moon and fly through the threshold to meet the Christ as his bride. This is the essence of a new matriarchal culture and a spiritual revolution in which the soul, as a hummingbird, discovers the beauty of life.

At the end of this book, I am walking through the Violet Forest, ending my personal life as I began, remembering that I first incarnated as a tree, later a hummingbird, and then symbolically as a centaur, and at last as a human being. Through this book, I have gone back to the past and died as a human being, resurrecting myself as a centaur to review the lessons of the paleolithic past, then as a hummingbird, my spirit, and last as a tree, the origin of life. I know when the last tree dies on Earth, we as humans will die. My hope is that we will enter the Violet Forest and resurrect a new culture to sustain life from the trees.

NOTES

INTRODUCTION

1. Nikos Kazantzakis, *Spain*, P. A. Bien, trans. (New York: Simon & Schuster, 1963).

PROLOGUE

1. Roger Shattuck, *The Banquet Years* (New York: Vintage Books, 1955, 1968).
2. Ibid.
3. Ibid.

CHAPTER 3

1. Robert Graves, *The White Goddess* (London: Faber & Faber, 1977).

CHAPTER 4

1. Theodore Roethke, *Collected Poems of Theodore Roethke* (New York: Doubleday, 1975).

CHAPTER 5

1. *Webster's Third New International Dictionary of the English Language Unabridged*, Philip Babcock, ed., (Springfield, MA: Merriam-Webster Inc., 1993).

CHAPTER 7

1. Kahlil Gibran, quoted in Meinrad Craighead, *The Sign of the Tree* (London: Artist House, Imprint Books, 1979).

CHAPTER 9

1. *Maori Creation Myth*, excerpted from Meinrad Craighead, *The Sign of the Tree*.

CHAPTER 14

1. George D. Mylonas, *Eleusis and the Eleusinian Mysteries* (Princeton, NJ: Princeton University Press, 1972).

BIBLIOGRAPHY

Barks, Coleman and John Moyne, *The Essential Rumi* (New York: Harper Collins, 1995).

Bisilliat, Maureen and Orlando and Claudio Villas-Boas, *Xingu— Tribal Territory* (São Paulo, Brazil: Cultura Editores Associado, 1990).

Blake, William, *The Urizen Books,* David Worral, ed. (Princeton, NJ: Princeton University Press, 1995).

Clow, Barbara Hand, *The Pleiadian Agenda* (Santa Fe, NM: Bear & Company, 1995).

Craighead, Meinrad, *The Sign of the Tree* (London: Artists House, Imprint Books, 1979).

Eliade, Mircae, *Images and Symbols* (London: Sheed & Ward, 1961).

Evans-Wentz, Walter, *The Tibetan Book of the Dead* (Oxford, England: Oxford University Press, 1974).

Graham, Laura G., *Performing Dreams: Discourses of Immortality Among Xavante of Central Brazil* (Austin, TX: University of Texas Press, 1995).

Graves, Robert, *The White Goddess* (London: Faber & Faber, 1977).

Hanh, Thich Nhat, *Living Buddha, Living Christ* (New York: G.P. Putnam, 1995).

Harner, Michael, *The Way of the Shaman* (San Francisco: Harper San Francisco, 1980).

Hixon, Lex, *Great Swan: Meetings with Ramakrishna* (New York: Larson Publications, 1992).

Homer, *Odyssey,* 2 vols. A.F. Garvic, ed. (Cambridge: Cambridge University Press, 1994).

Jonas, Hans, *The Gnostic Religion: The Message of the Alien God and the Beginnings of Christianity,* 2nd ed.(Boston: Beacon Press, 1963).

Kazantzakis, Nikos, *Spain,* P. A. Bien, trans. (New York: Simon & Schuster, 1963).

Kryder, Rowena Pattee, *The Faces of the Moon Mother* (Mt. Shasta, CA: Golden Point Productions, 1991).

Leviton, Richard, *The Imagination of Pentecost* (Hudson, NY: Anthroposophic Press, 1994).

Mylonas, George D., *Eleusis and the Eleusinian Mysteries* (Princeton, NJ: Princeton University Press, 1972).

Ott, Jonathon, *Ayahuasca Analogues: Pangaen Ethneogens* (Kennewick, WA: Natural Products Co., 1994).

Patanjali, *Yoga-Sutra*, George Feuerstein, trans. (Rochester, VT: Inner Traditions, 1989).

Prokofieff, Sergei, *Rudolf Steiner and the Founding of the New Mysteries* (London: Rudolf Steiner Press, 1986).

Rao, K.N., *Yogis, Destiny and the Wheel of Time* (Lucknow, India: Vani Graphics, 1995).

Reinhart, Melanie, *Chiron and the Healing Journey* (London: Penguin Books, 1989).

Reyo, Zulma, *Mastery: The Path of Inner Alchemy* (London: Janus Publishing Company, 1994).

Sansonese, J. Nigro, *The Body of Myth* (Rochester, VT: Inner Traditions International, 1994).

Shattuck, Roger, *The Banquet Years* (New York: Vintage Books, 1955, 68).

Steiner, Rudolf, *Ancient Myths and the New Isis Mystery* (Hudson, NY: Anthroposophic Press, 1994).

Steiner, Rudolf, *Christ in Relation to Lucifer and Ahriman* (Spring Valley, NY: Anthroposophic Press, 1978).

Steiner, Rudolf, *Cosmic Memory: Prehistory of Earth and Man* (New York: Harper and Row, 1981).

Steiner, Rudolf, *The Ahrimanic Deception* (Spring Valley, NY: Anthroposophic Press, 1988).

Steiner, Rudolf, *The Mission of Archangel Michael*. 2nd Ed. (Spring Valley, NY: Anthroposophic Press, 1961).

Tyrrell, Robert A. and Esther Quesada, *Hummingbirds: Their Life and Behavior* (New York: Crown Publishers, 1985).

Wilhelm, Richard ed., *The Secret of the Golden Flower*: A Chinese Book of Life (New York: Harcourt Brace, 1988).

ABOUT THE AUTHOR

Foster Perry is a teacher of a new kind of self-healing—*Hummingbird Healing Work*—using soul therapy and the healing nature of sound, movement, and bodywork. It is a spiritual science of healing on all levels. He is a graduate of Georgetown University, and is the author of *When Lightning Strikes a Hummingbird*. His international workshops have taken him to over twenty countries, and he leads Medicine Journeys to ancient sacred sites around the world. Foster is the president of the Hummingbird Foundation based in Santa Fe, New Mexico with offices in London and Brazil. With his partner, Eugenia Lyras, he is planning to build a spiritual retreat and spa for education in the healing and spiritual arts in New Mexico.